FRANK HÖHNE
THE BOOK OF BOCK

gestalten

PRELUDE

by Hugo Höhne,
Streetmusician,
Idol &
Grandfather of this book.
And
Maybe the only person who learned english
in Neugersdorf (Gierschdurf) in the roaring 60s.

THANK YOU
For supporting my book:

HELGA ⎫
HUGO ⎪
CHARLOTTE ⎬ HÖHNE + LARS Böhnke, STADT Wesel, DOMINIK Arbach, TOBI Röttger, STEFAN Wunderwald, JONAS Natterer, SZYMON Flachtinowitz, FLO Sänger, MACKAN Ekroth, SEBASTIAN Haslover, Bernd Trautvetter, NANNE Meyer, MANFRED Vogel, Sarah WILLE, Majus WEN KER, JULLE Burchard, SAMIR Omar, TIMM Sonnenschein, The HORT and all those people that I forgot although they made my days here and there, like Cashiers, Doctors etc.
KRISTIN ⎪
JUDITH ⎭

AND MOST OF ALL
THANK YOU: <u>OLIVIA + MATILDA</u>

(I am crying while writing your names, I love you)

Dear Frank!   2012, April 26.

By phone I heard today, that you will publish a new book. Well done!

If a man got a job, wich is also his obsession, so he is a lucky guy. I don't know much about your work, because I hate the digital-world. I don't use modern communication-equipment. That's why I can't look at your home-page. But the modern digital bullshit wastes a lot of Life-time from our young generation.

I don't know, if some people will love your book. I don't know, if you will get some money with your book. But I know, that you love to paint, to write and to be a creating man. For everybody, that could spend his live with a work he love, the clock-wringing in the morning is a beautiful noise. And when other people will love your work too, so it's a very big gift. And don't forget: Too much money is toxic! Take a look at the destroyed people at Wall-street. For the most of them it'll be better to paint pictures. So they may be saved from hell.

Watch your family! It's more important than books or money. Watch your health! Drink wine, eat much garlic and have fun. So you will survive 100 jears.

God bless you!
your father Honky Tonk Hugo

hi,

THIS IS ME ↓

→ FRANK HÖHNE
→ freelance ILLUSTRATOR
  from BERLIN/Europe
→ writing to YOU (I wish)

about BOCK

because:
»die GESTALTEN« came up to me asking if I had BOCK to make a book with »die GESTALTEN«. OF COURSE I HAVE BOCK. So this BOOK is a BOCKumentation about me, FRANK HÖHNE, that One In A Million Illustrator from EARTH.

* btw.

bock

is a german expression for

1. → billy-goat

and

2. **Lust**

both suit me but think of LUST when I use that word BOCK in this BOOK, ok? bock?

for **Life**

follow your
HeART
when you look

a pity-pity drawing of IGGY

for your
DAY JOB   because →

So look for a
job YOU might

have BO C K for >

FOR the rest of
r OUR life!
but what kind of WORK is cool
since the coalmines shut down in
GERMANY/EUROPE?

Cover for FLUTER "ARBEIT", 2010

FIND YOUR JOB

I.

YOU FEEL TOO
UGLY
TO HAVE A
"FACE to FACE" - JOB
in an office?

AND II.

and III.
you feel like doing BIG business from HOME?

LAND DER UMSETZUNG

EINE FABRIK IN GUANGDONG

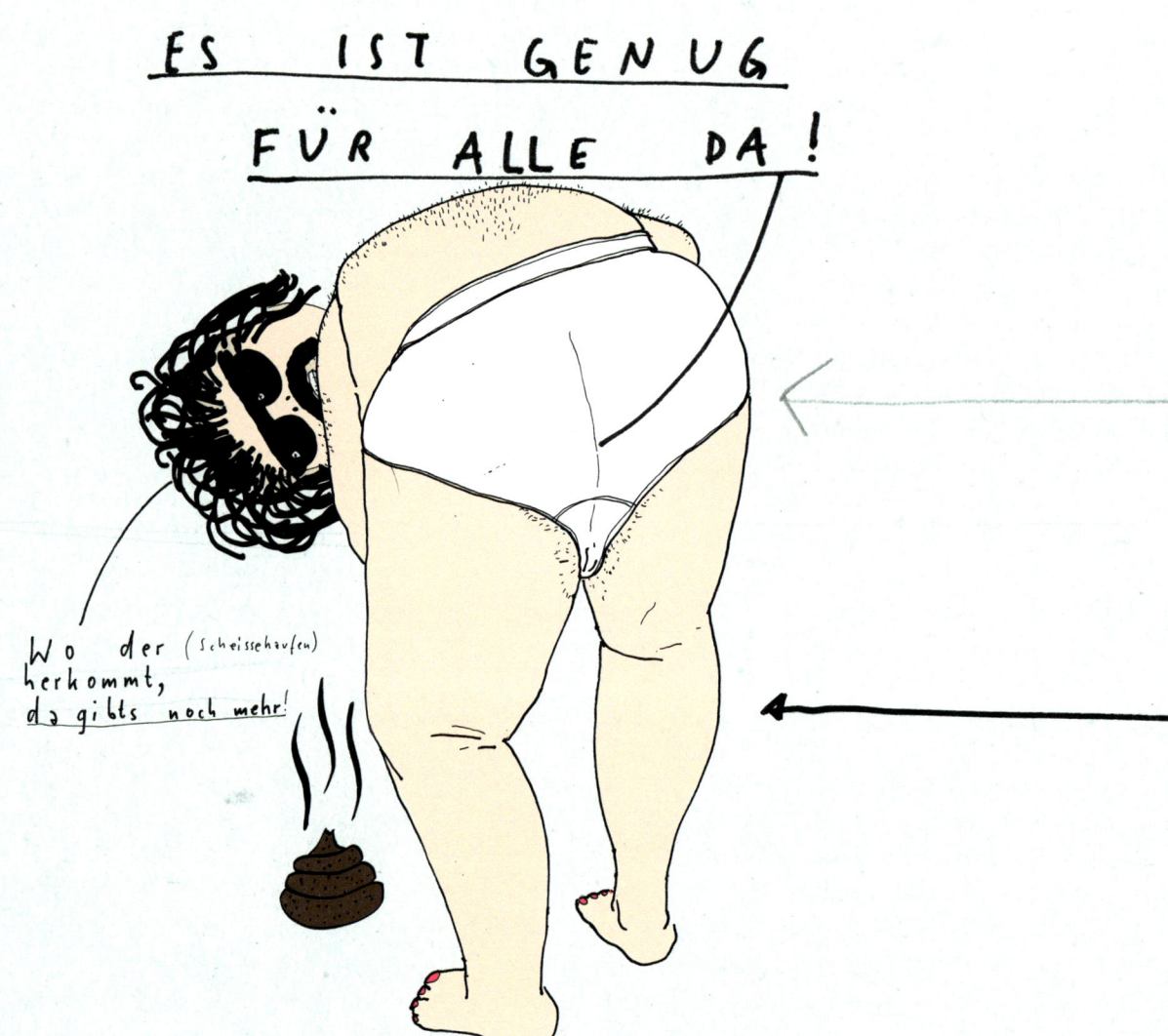

and V.

YOU THINK

THIS IS FUNNY?

OR NOT.
but it is funny, right?
yeah, it's funny, isn't IT?
DON'T YOU THINK THAT THIS IS FUNNY?

if you do not think that this is really, I mean REALLY FUNNY, PUT THIS BOOK AWAY, BECAUSE IT WON'T GET ANY FUNNIER.

THEN:

YOU

definitely

have B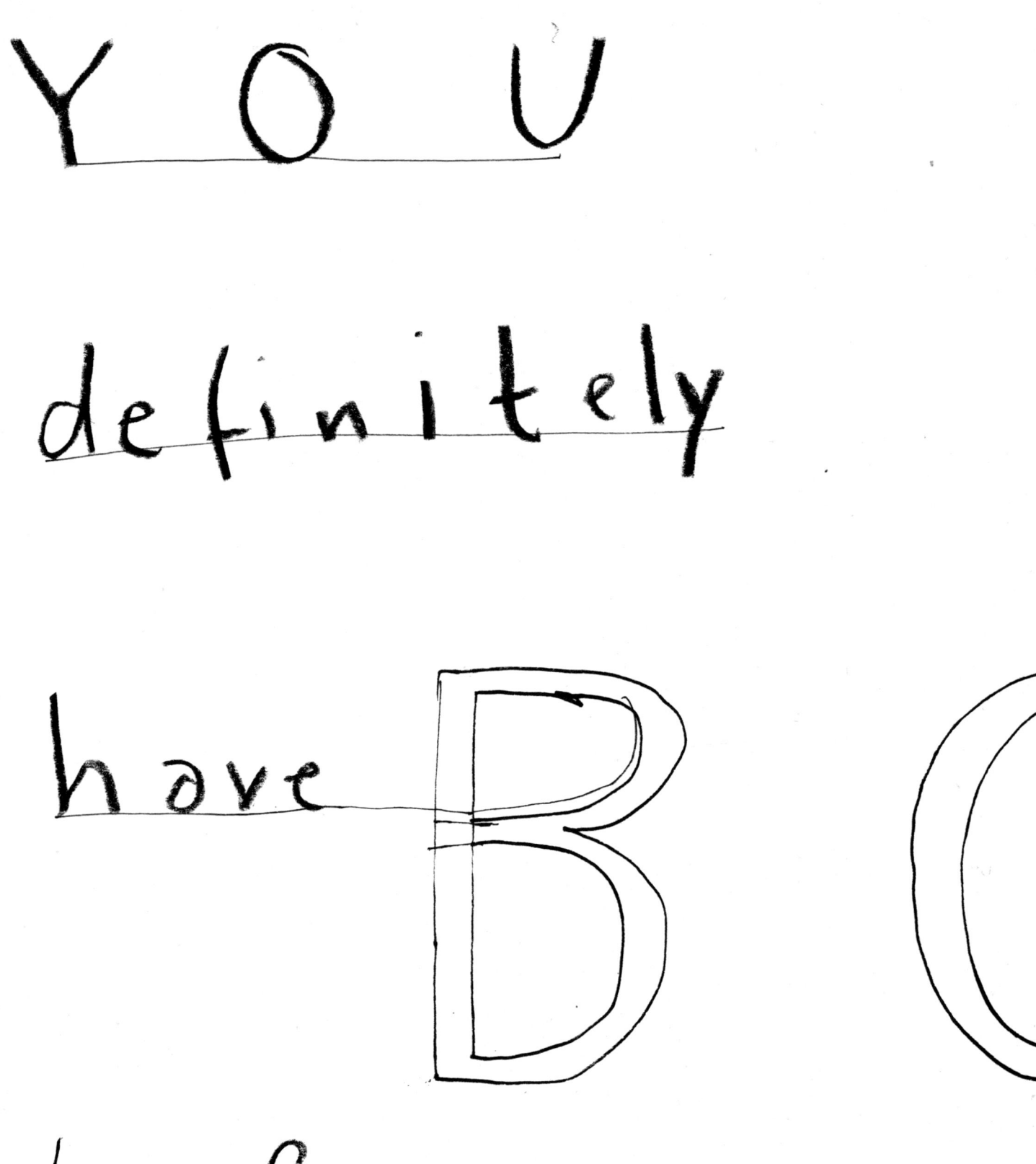

to br another

OCK
→ illustRATOR

OK.
ILLUST
OK. OK OK!
~~SURE?~~

WHAT THE HECTOR ~~tries~~ does this DOUBLE-PAGE pretend to be?

RATOR

OK- fine.

Okay
but why?
ok.
OK
getting →

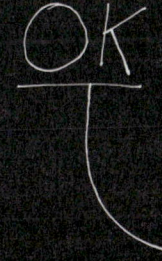

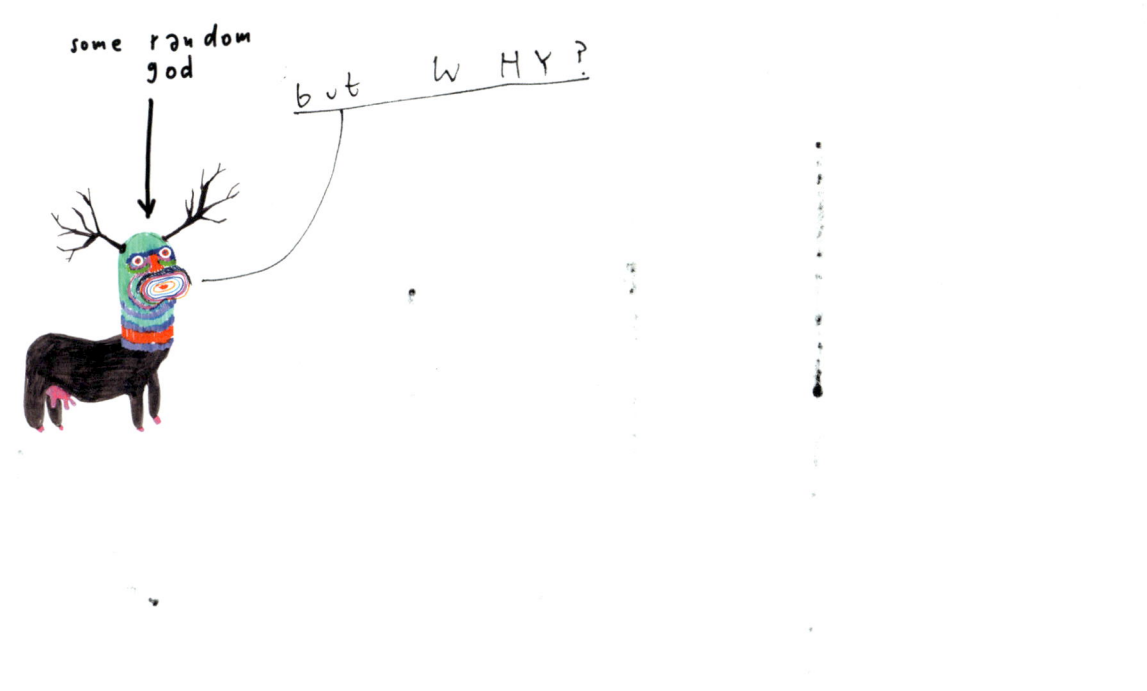

some random god

but WHY?

BECAUSE

if you have too much (money) you don't appreciate anything and won't develop ~~time~~ the PASSION for

it is there ~~your~~ and always ~~parents feed you~~ was and seemingly will be there for ~~all~~ your life

→ **INSPIRATION** ←

some random rich person

but why?

Annie Lennox

THE INSPIRATION

WHOOAH, psychedelic, huh?!

'is YOUR
OWN **BLOOD**
YOUR LIFE
ALL YOUR EXPERIENCEs

THE MORE YOU'VE GONE THROUGH
[whether GOOD or BAD]
THE MORE
inspiration runs through your VEINS.

just like ELVIS.   ¿what? quando quando   SO

live your
LIFE

FILL IT UP ↓

with as much trial (T) & ERROR as you can.

Live IT HARD
FE

HOWDY—
I am new in this BOOK,
BUT WHAT DOES
»REAL LIFE EXPERIENCE« HAVE TO DO WITH <u>MONEY</u>,
<u>STUPIDO</u>?!

QUICK EXAMPLE
WHY MONEY SUCKS UP YOUR RANDOM "RICH" KID

Want to go GOLFING

&LATTE

BROS

← V

I WANT IT
I GET IT

Drives his fancy car to golf course → plays golf → goes home

Experience POINTS = 1 PT

INSPIRATION
CREATIVITY
EXPERIENCE

REALLY COOL KID

THIS is MY very BFF LARS.

GeÖÖÖLfing?

random BOCK BEER

S →

HAVE NO IDEA IF I WANT IT, BUT

I TRY = BOCK

- never had a car
  → hitchhikes to the countryside
  → the driver is a prostitute (CLASSIC)
  → ~~cool kid never met a prostitute before~~
  → ~~really enjoys dead~~
  , it's christmas,
  → after exchanging ringtones prostitute drops kid off at the golf course
  → kid climbs the fence
  → kid gets in trouble with the security guards, alarmed by the "rich" kid, seeing "cool" kid sneaking over the fence
  → cool kid ~~decides~~ gets into a fight with the caddy of cool kid, after climbing the fence again he'd have preferred to beat up rich kid but rich kid hides in the ~~car~~ club house
  → cool kid has been cuffed when mother picks him up at the local police station

Experience POINTS = 18 pts

THE POINT

when you are wealthy: YOUR LIFE STINKS. YOUR HAPPINESS HAS DISAPPOINTING HOLES YOU THINK MONEY CAN FILL. BUT BIGGER MONEY = BIGGER HOLES. =

NOT HAPPY

IS ☐ TWO
▓ ☐ WORDS:

Cheese People

TIME GOES BY and ~~into the thing~~ WASTE ~~stupid~~
YOU ~~spend~~ IT WITH FIXING YOUR HOLES.

less ↓

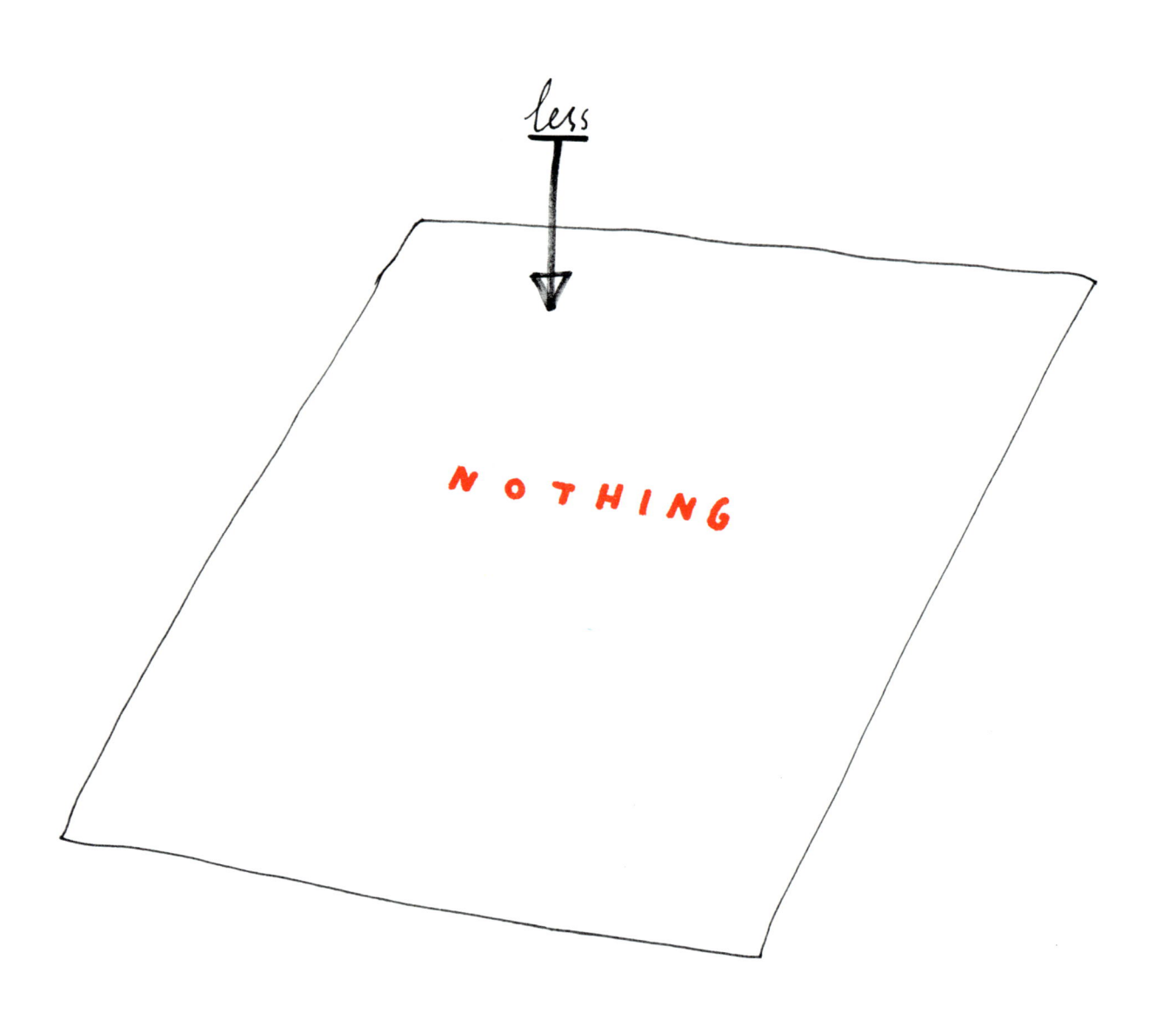

NOTHING

= MORE

nothing

means

let's PLAY!

CReativity!

wow that's deep

OF COURSE

IT'S

do you understand that the GUY on the page before puts his finger right here on this page deep into THIS BULLSHIT and said "that's deep"

BULLSHIT

and you thought he meant that crap on the page before but he means this turd here this literal bull-shit is literally deep and he tests its depth with his finger. funny, right?

WHAT I

SAID

ABOUT

THE

RICH

BUT

isn't it's a fact:

the coolest people grew up in simplicity.

THE HONESTY OF WORKING CLASS: PEOPLE WHO SUFFER ARE MOTIVATED to create WAYS OUT OF THERE. TO CHANGE THEIR WORLD.

BACK
hYWAY,
TO
BO

CK ⬇ getting started as an illustrator.

1. INSPIRATION SHOULD BE YOUR LIFE, SO FILL IT UP!

2. DRAW

FORTUNE TELLER PAGE

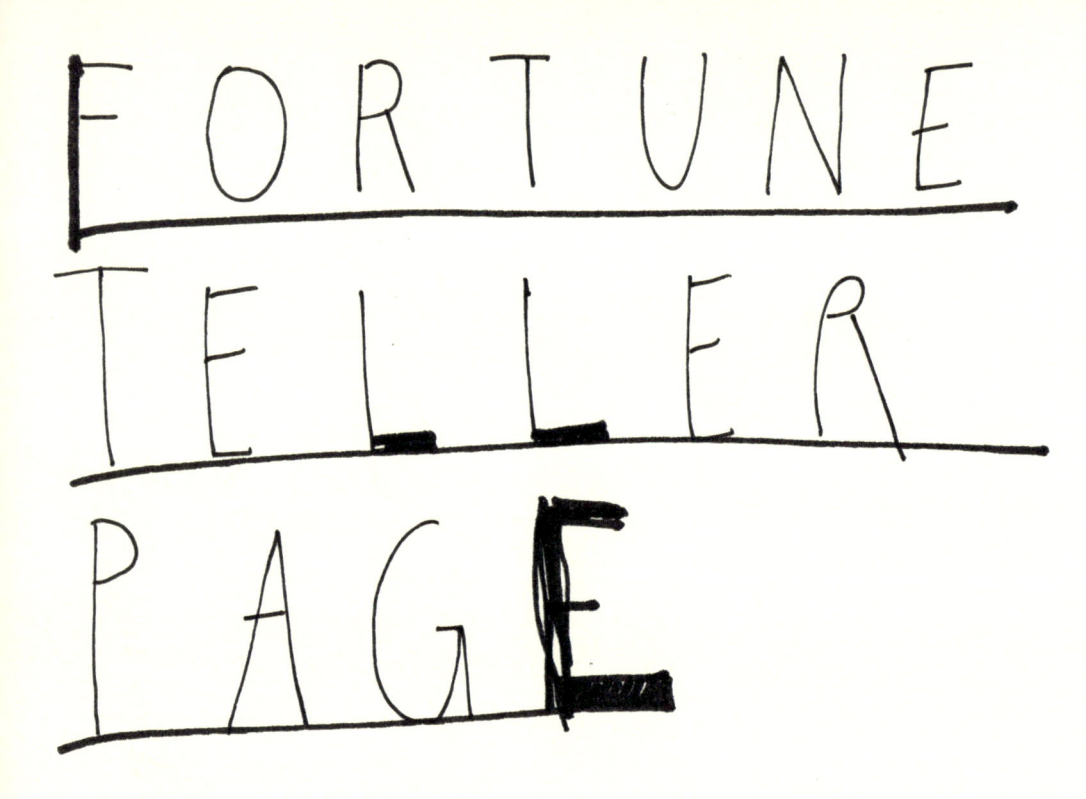

———————————————————————▶

TAKE A PHOTO
and send it to
IDREWANELEPHANT@FRANKHOEHNE.DE.

↑
draw an elephant with a headache

OK. does it look like this?

Latoya Jackson

ASPIRIN

You're gonna make a lot of money in ADVERTISING BUT have trouble sleeping.

or this

Jennifer Rush

it is WRONG!

YOU'RE GONNA WORK FOR POLITICAL FOUNDATIONS make enough money to survive BUT WILL FEEL RIGHT-HEARTED.

OR LIKE THIS?

Renate Künast

OUCH MY HEAD, GRROAARRRR

hmm. i guess you're gonna make it in that mysterious comic-scene

OR ?

Dolf Lundgren

You do your own thing. SCREENPRINTS, T-SHIRTS, MOUSEPADS, ...

OR MORE like this?

Pope

CLASSIC.

YOUR FRIENDS LIKE YOUR BIRTHDAY CARDS. BUT THAT'S PRETTY MUCH IT.

OR THIS?

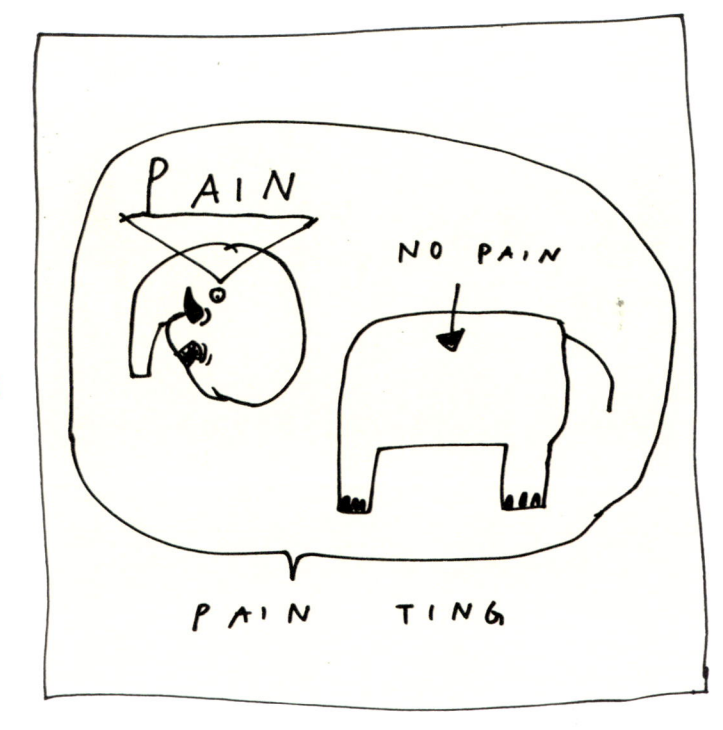

Richard Grieco

eerm... interesting, yes... eerm.

OR LIKE THIS?

Christina Uglyera

puhh. WHO SAID you're allowed to use colours?

JUST DRAW IF YOU HAVE BOCK.

POINT IS. ~~YOU~~ JUST BECAUSE MAYBE YOU CAN DRAW — IT'S THE IDEA NOT THE SKILLS THAT MATTER. SKILLS ARE OVERRATED. A CAMERA COSTS 30€ THESE DAYS. WHY DRAWING?

BOCK in Illustration is the only aspect that matters. BECAUSE THE BOCK YOU HAVE MAKING an ILLUSTRATION TRANSPORTs BOCK into THE OBSERVER.

Illustrators are visual <u>storytellers</u>. here comes »Live your life« again. You need to have stories to tell...

IT'S only ENTERTAINMENT.

THE ART OF ENTERTAINMENT
EXAMPLE:

A GUY WALKS BY.

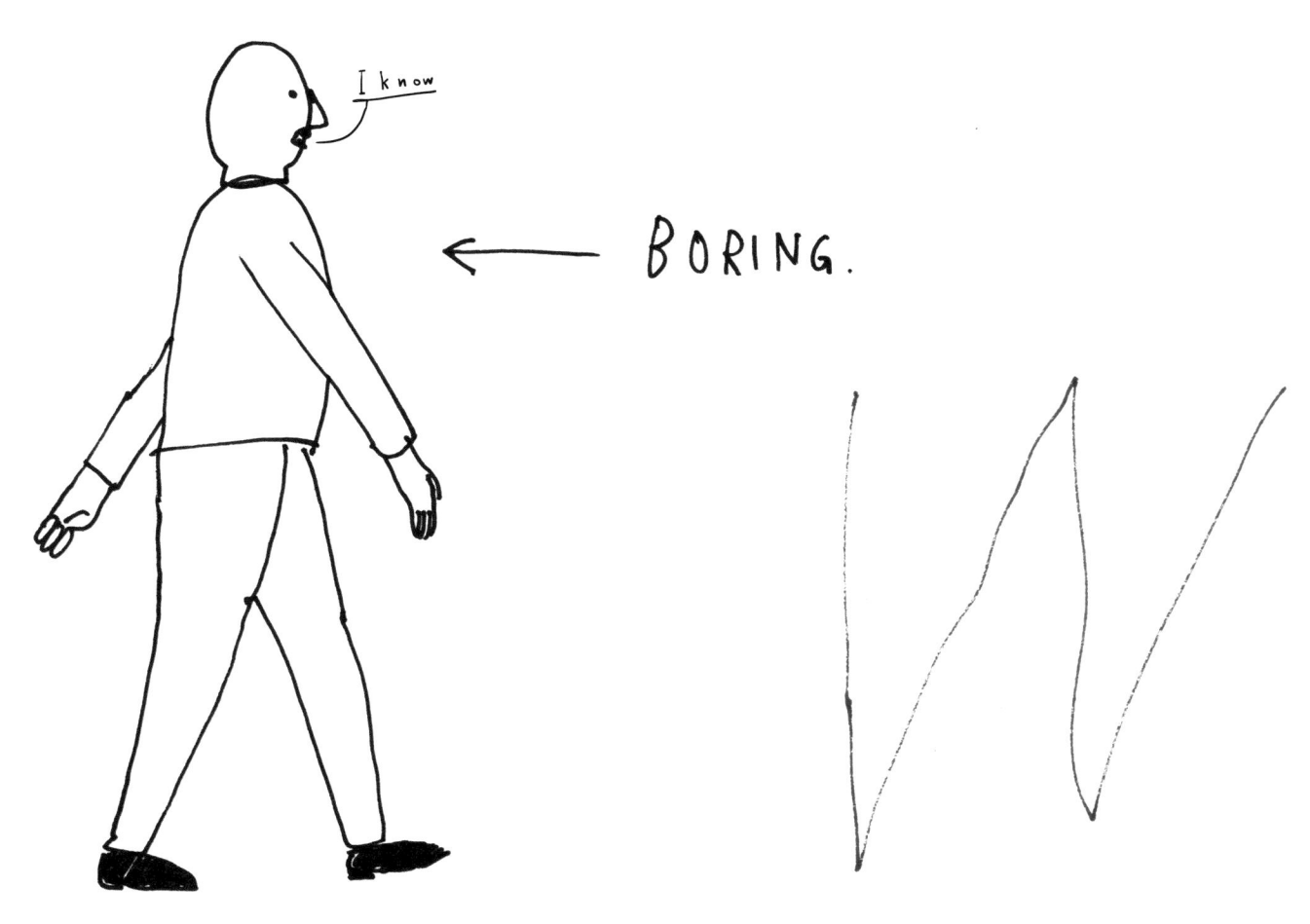

"I know"

← BORING.

THIS GUY CAN WALK. HE'S BEEN WALKING FOR DECADES. NOTHING SPECIAL ABOUT THAT WALK.

FAILURE = INDIVIDUAL CHARACTER FIGHTING THE PERFECT

A KID WALKS BY.

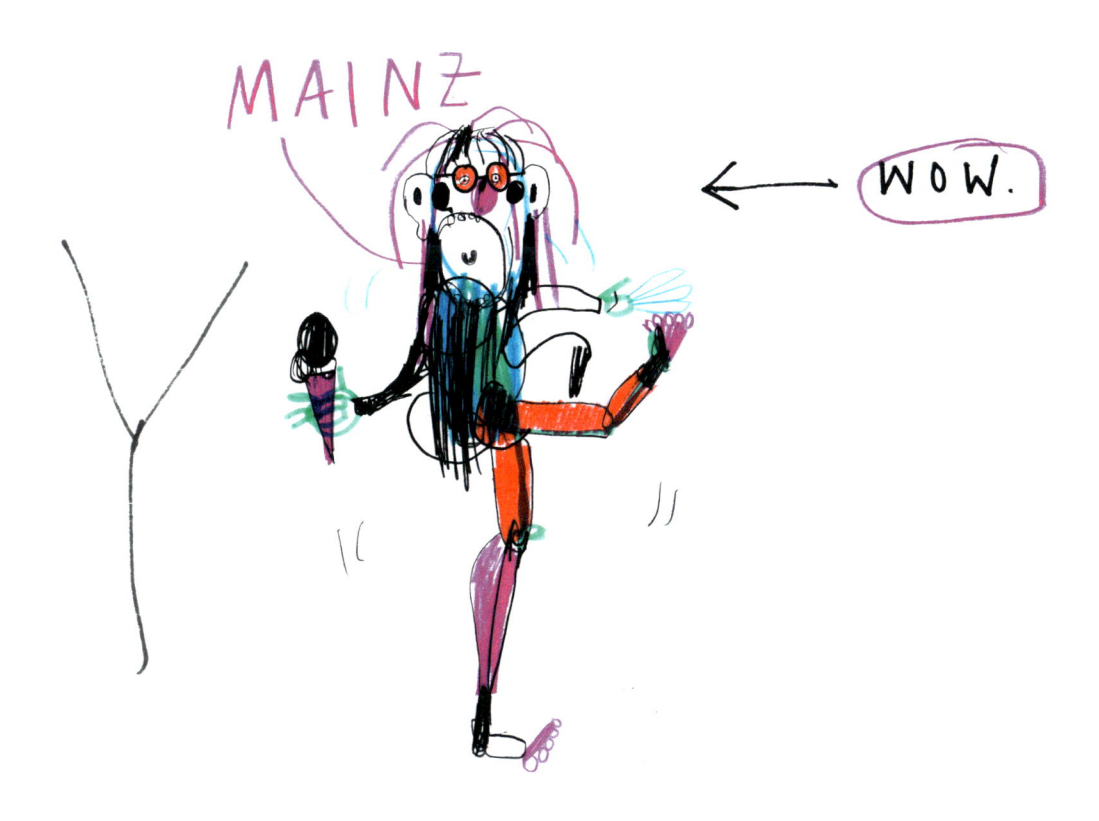

MAINZ ← WOW.

HY?

THIS KID JUST LEARNED TO WALK.
HE'S ALMOST ABOUT TO FALL. BUT HE IS SO HAPPY AND PROUD.
YOU JUST WANT TO WATCH AND SEE WHAT HAPPENS NEXT.
IT'S SURPRISING → IT'S ENTERTAINING IN ITS UNPERFECTNESS.

THIS B
is
So lame

OOK

i assume:

YOU are in the book shop right now, browsing a bit, picked up this book of what the ~~fuck~~ Buck, don't know me, realized that this guy's english is pretty bad, ~~and~~ but even worse is what he tries to explain... and you are about to put this book away, because you ~~would see~~ thought it was a picturebook.

You want visual entertainment.

I mean, so ~~I~~ (now on this monday the 19th of May 2012) decided to give up on theories and just draw and arrange some pictures THAT ARE SUPPOSED TO PROVE THAT I HAVE BOCK.

PICKLE FUCK

WENKEN

SITUATION?

POLITICS

CTRL+A

DEL

YEAH

SPIPIT

last night a **Currywurst** *saved my life*

iiiieh!

DAS ~~ZDF~~ ~~AHNSTEIN~~ HAT MICH STARK GEMACHT.

KERZ

15 IV → heu

te is echt HART.

EY DIESE ARME SIND SO KOOL
TOTAL, ACHTE ICH MACH DIE HOCH EY, KOOL
EY FREUNDE, TSCHEKKT DAS!
AUF

WEB 2.0

EGO GOTT

LSD.

WIEVIEL Hättste deNN gern? *felicità*

ES
05

VERFRIEND REQ

HAPP
NESS

orphydra

&

STOP
THE
WHORE

SCHUTT

58 ich steh auf Speck ham spr1

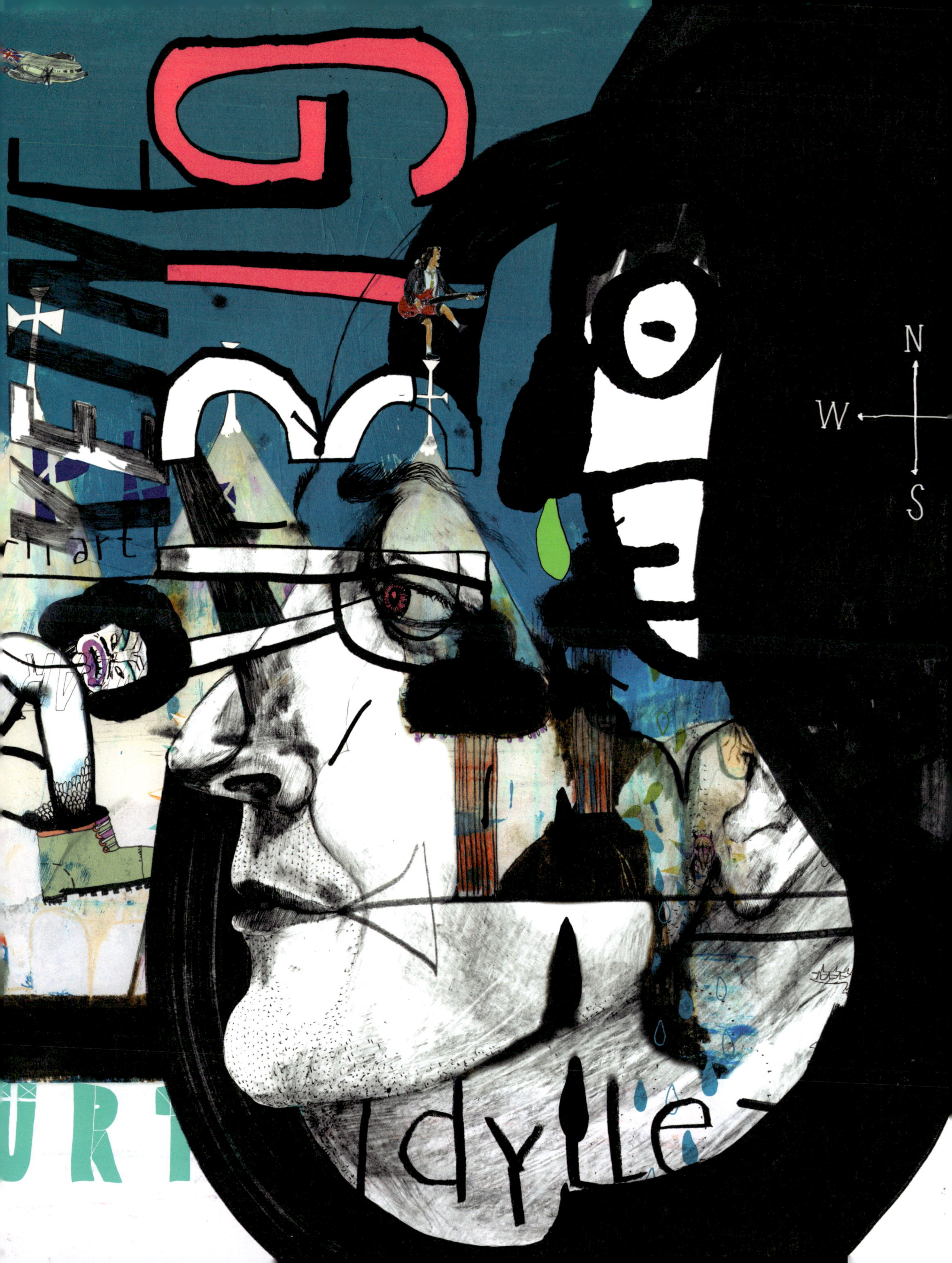
N
W
S
art
dylle

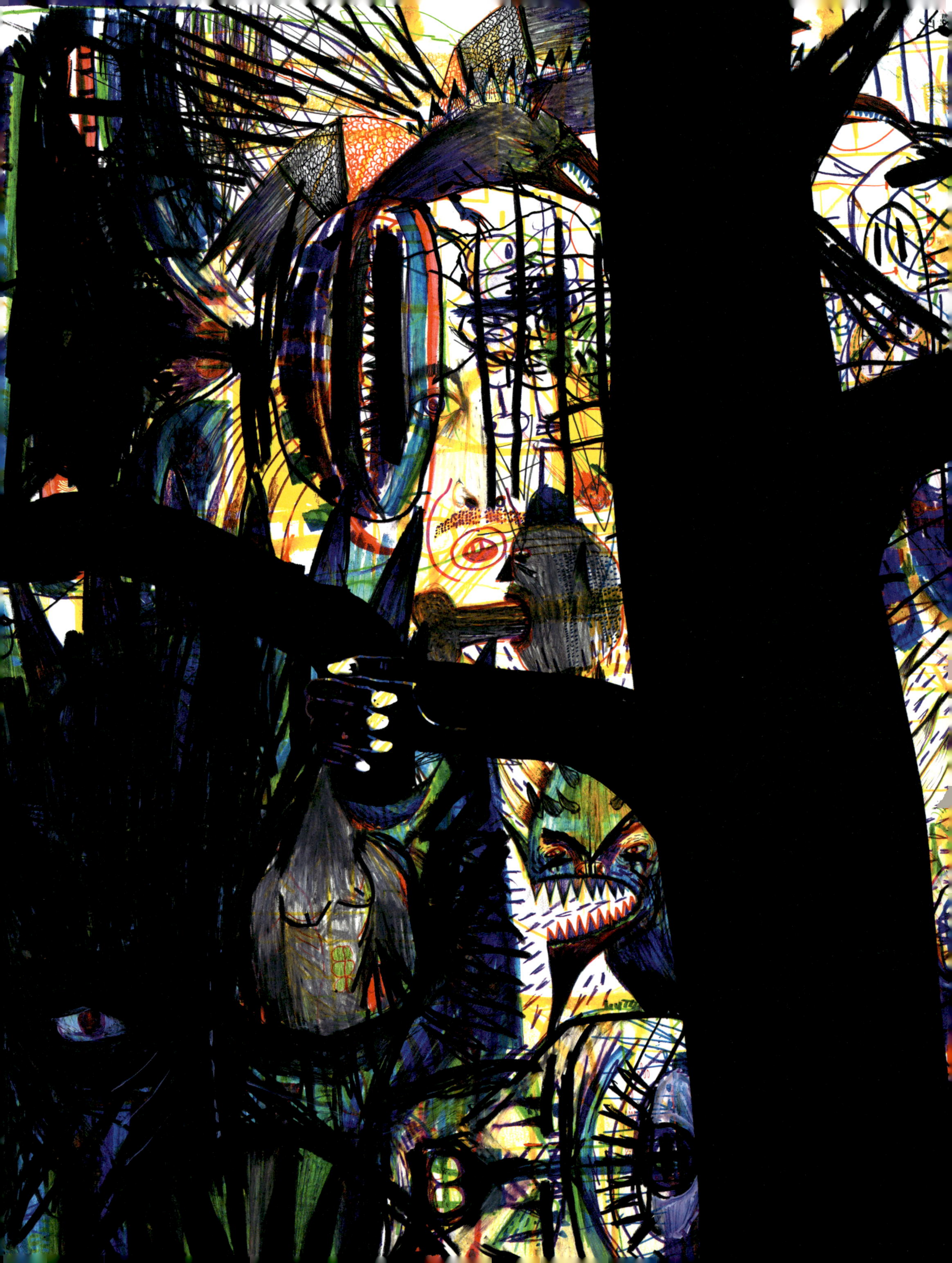

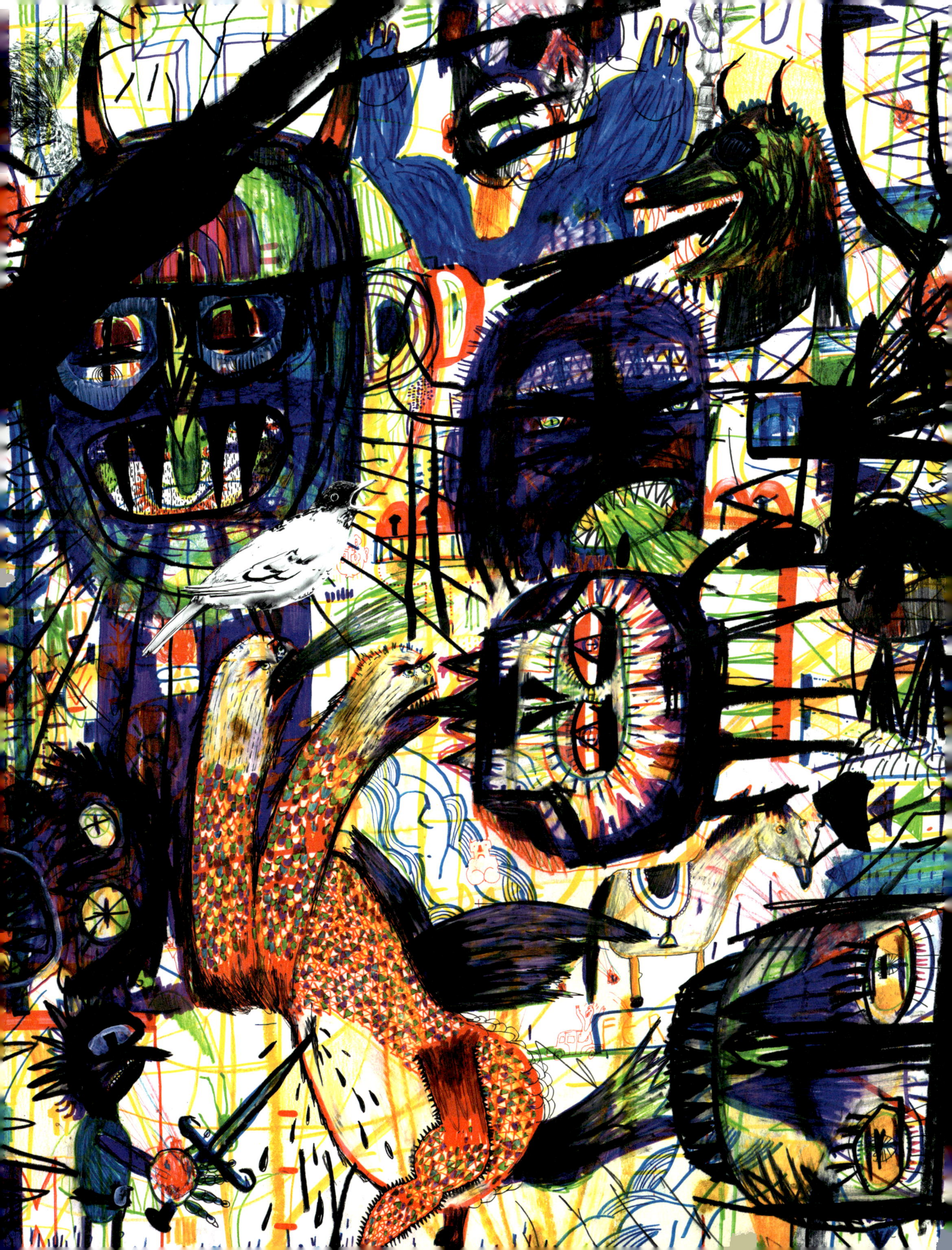

ICH BIN das MITTELMAß
und sowas von VOLL, EY

MAYBE
WITH
SEHEN
ICH HABE M
17 ZIGARETTEN 3,90€
GRÜNDE?
WEISS
Rauchen macht sterblich
Made in the EU
Teer 6 mg Nikotin 0,5 mg Kohlen-monoxid 8 mg

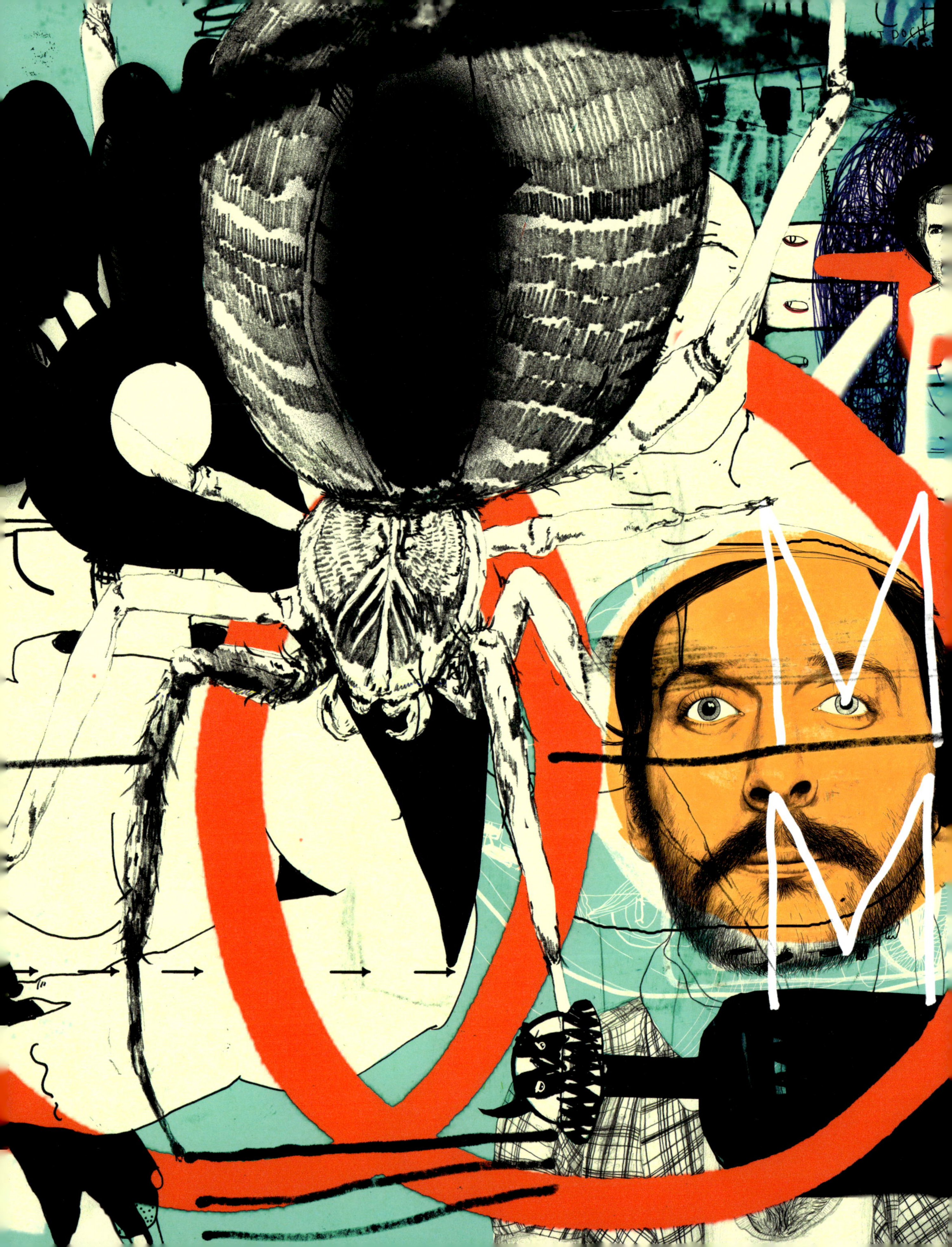
M
M

KRAUFALL!
Gebirgskette
ICH SACH MA SO: GOTT SAVE THE QUEER, ALTA
05
ARRY
FAMALT
ANGST

OK

sure thong, I could have put more energy in this DRAWING, but I HAD NO ROCK.

illustration is moody, so be <u>honest</u> and <u>work</u> <u>how you feel</u>.

Enough with meaningless pic-salads.

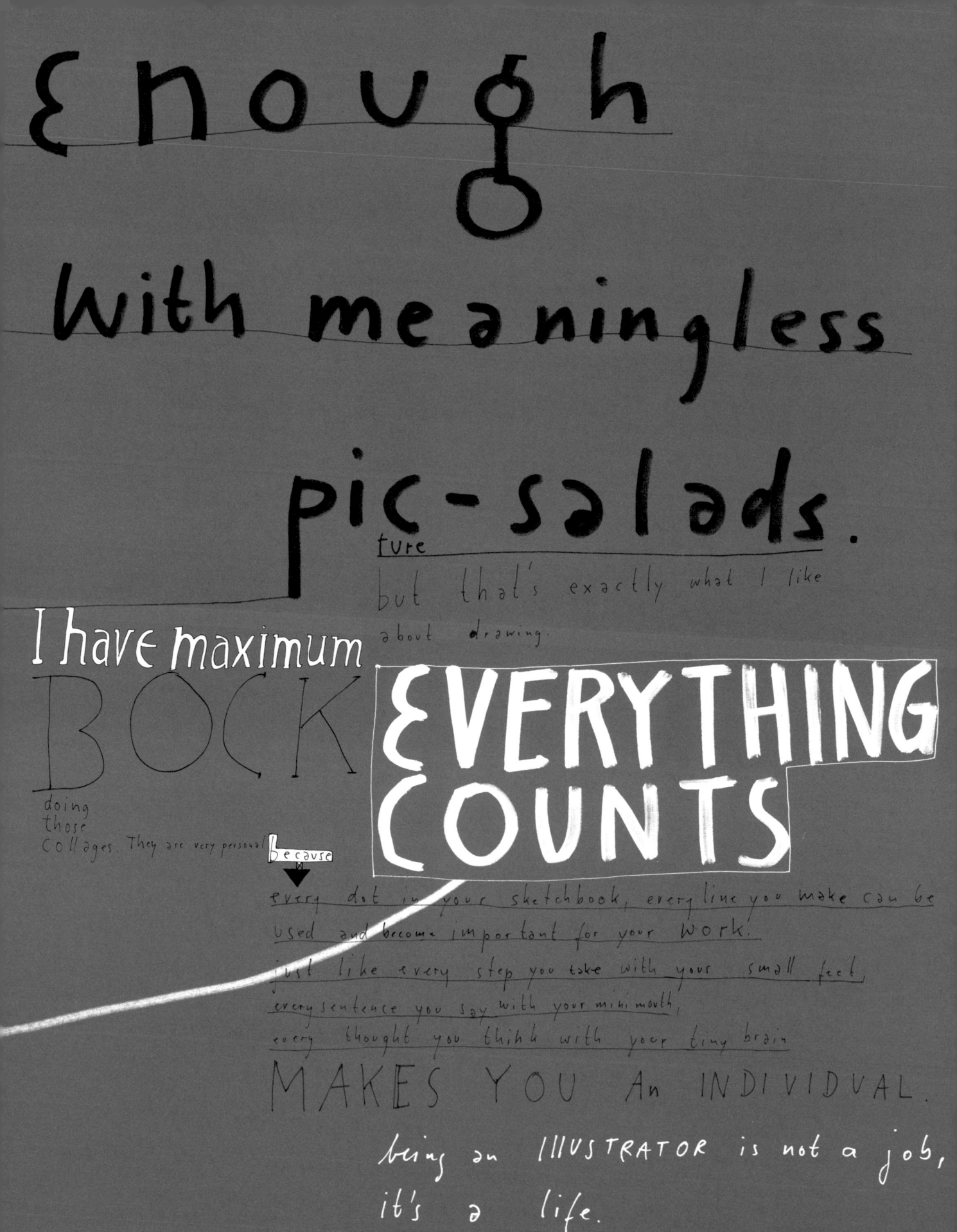

ture

but that's exactly what I like about drawing.

I have maximum BOCK doing those collages. They are very personal because

EVERYTHING COUNTS

every dot in your sketchbook, every line you make can be used and become important for your work. just like every step you take with your small feet, every sentence you say with your mini mouth, every thought you think with your tiny brain MAKES YOU An INDIVIDUAL.

being an ILLUSTRATOR is not a job, it's a life.

BACK TO BOO
nynon,

1. INSPIRATION is E~~X~~PERIMENTING with LIFE
2. DRAW
3. → MAKING IT A JOB.

GEt COM

little Money FOR

FORT KNOX able with

A WHILE -

maybe even L⚬NG⚬nger. hooray

earn enough money to survive
with lousy ~~side jobs~~ LIKE →

BEING AN EXTRA FOR A TV-SERIES.

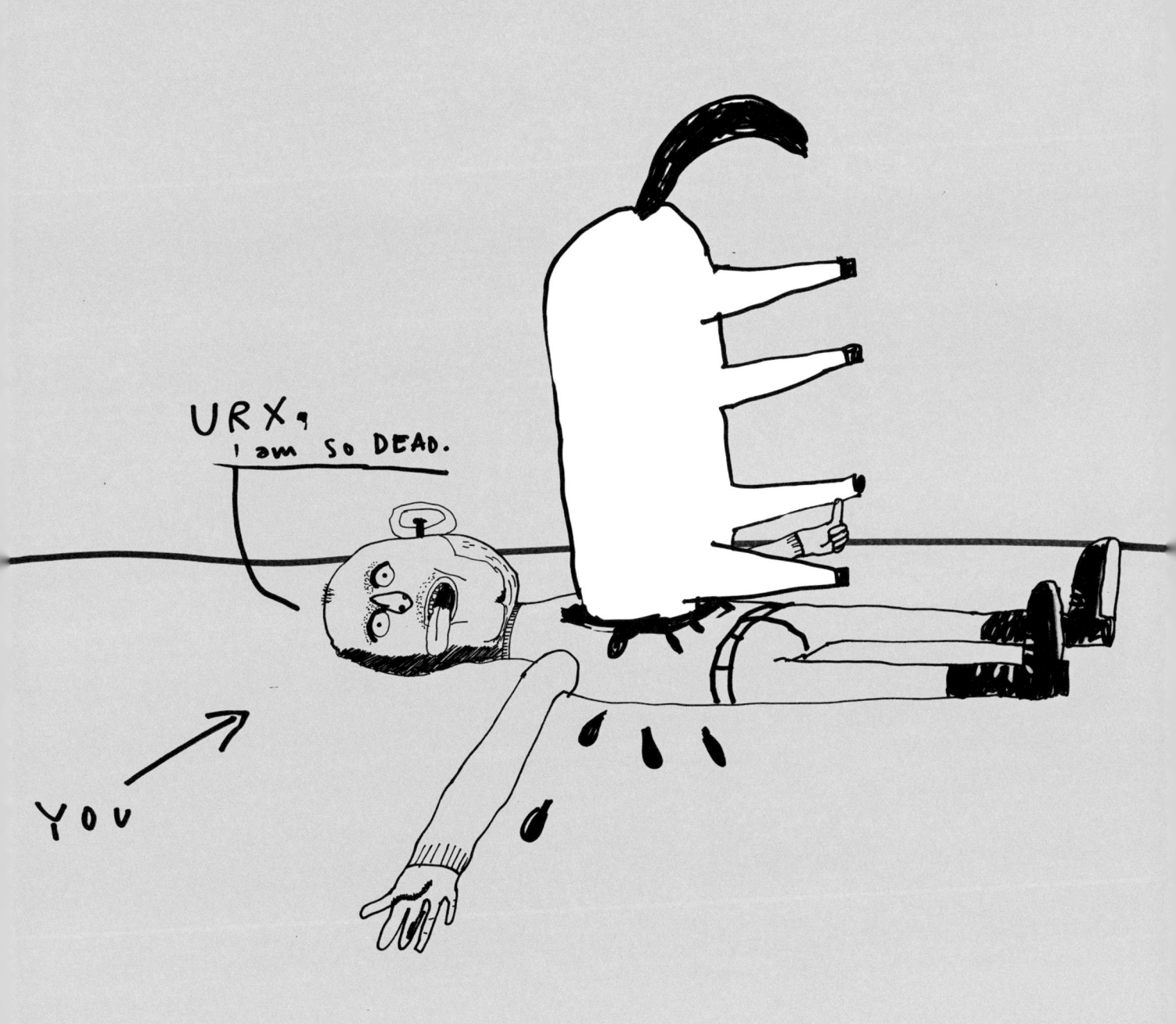

URX, i am so DEAD.

YOU

"HORSEKILLER, YOU SON OF A DUTCH."

← STAR OF THE SHOW

BEING AN AGENT IN A CALL CENTER

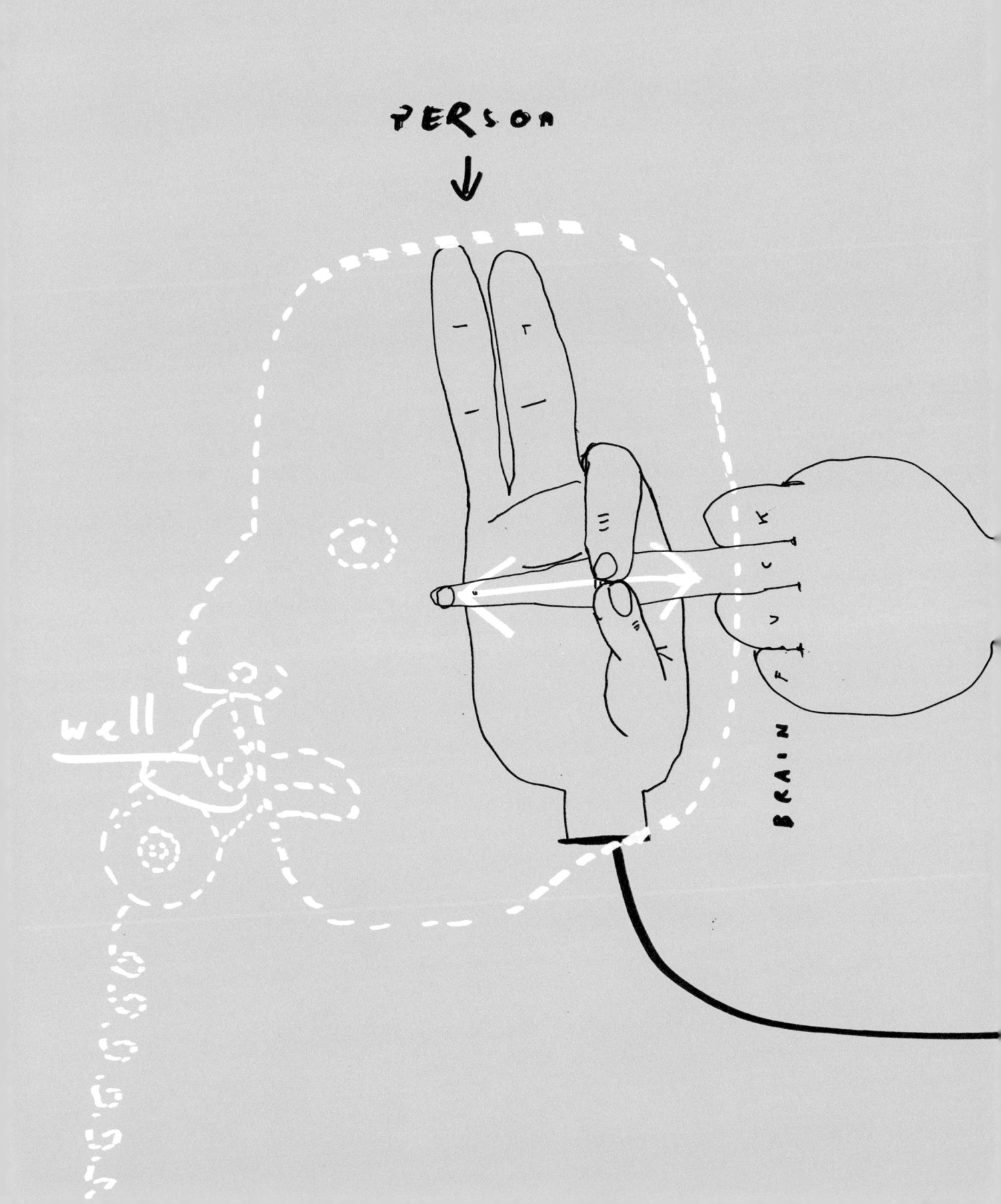

PERSON ↓

well

BRAIN

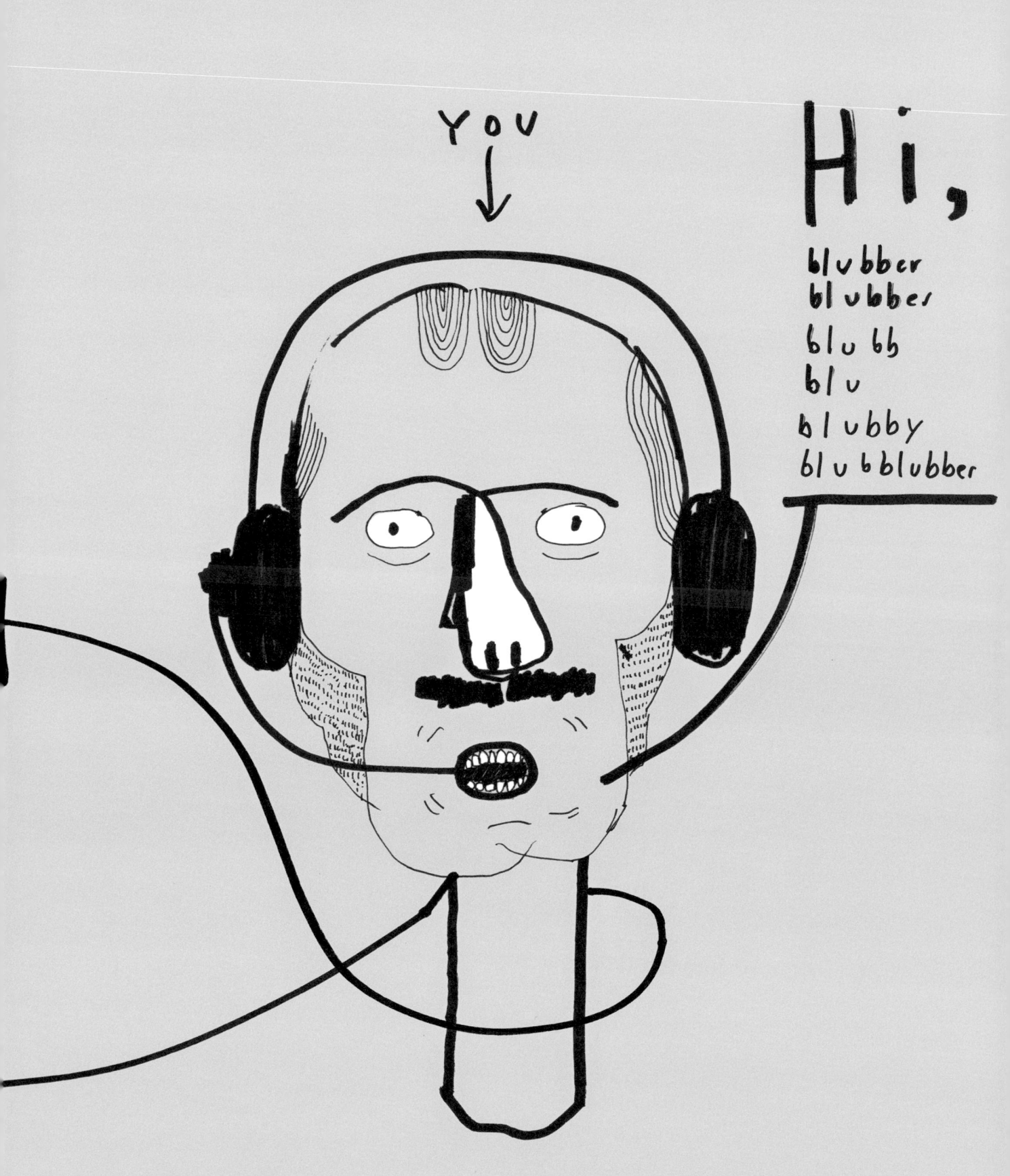

↓ YOU

Hi,
blubber
blubbes
blubb
blu
blubby
blubblubber

BEING A BARTENDER

SCHNAPS

← You

peep

GReurrl

IT REALLY WHAT YOU PICK ASS LONG AS

rofl, a nickel

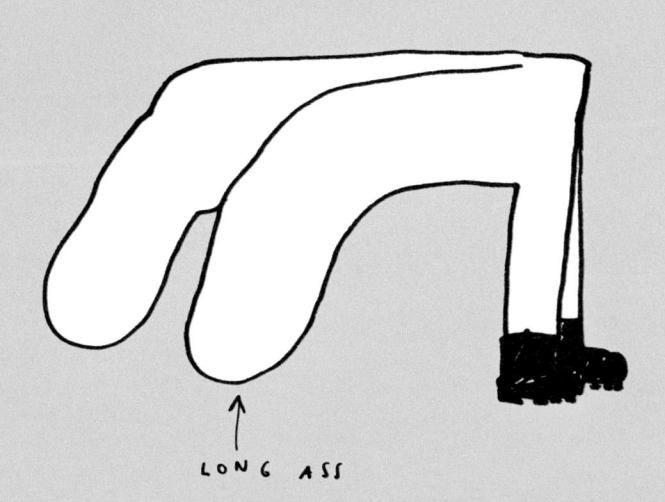

↑ LONG ASS

DOESN'T MATTER JOB

it pays your RENT + FOOD and you can simultaneously fill your sketchbook with bock

21x
Denken rettet!
K
S
T
K
Machst Du das öfters?
Jopp!
FAKÉ
HEY → HEY
WANKERS
057/OK
EGOESSTISCH
Bon

PSSECHBOOKS

WHILE DAYJOBBING HARD.

SKE
ARE
DUMPS

BOOKS FOR INSPIRATION.

YOU CAN ALWAYS USE ANY OF YOUR DRAWINGS TO REARRANGE YOUR PLAYGROUND.

So:
- DRAW
- SCAN →

SH8OW IT!

HTTP://YOUR Home PAGE

SHOW IT ALL.
EVEN THINGS THAT YOU MAY THINK SUCK.

THINK GLOBAL.
THERE IS DEFINITELY SOMEONE ONLINE THAT THINKS LOL, YOU ARE KILLER! → although you

NOT BAD — NOT BAD AT ALL

Browsing your HP ↓

UPLOADING: ALL THE CRAP!....
CANCEL CLOSE

ITALY

THIS IS NATTORIUS B.I.G., GERMANY'S ART DIRECTOR WITH THE MOST IMPACT ON MY LITTLE GENERATION

TINK — BUT WHY SHOULD YOU CARE AS LONG AS PEOPLE ARE ENTERTAINED.

ALL OF A SUDDEN, AFTER DAYS, MONTHS, YEARS OF WAITING ONLINE: SOME EDITOR or so WRITES AN ANGRY EMAIL asking WHY YOU HAVEN'T WORKED WITH HIM YET. SO YOU ANSWER:

SORRY, ANDI RICHTER, I'll CHANGE AND

ET VOILÀ (?)
YOUR FIRST JOB FOR VICE MAGAZINE. NOTHING TO BE PROUD OF, BUT <u>good ENOUGH for ME</u> *

JAMBOE
WE NEED ANOTHER NEW YORK POST PUNK NO-WAVE SCENE. BLOODY HELL!

* ALSO MONEYWISE. 50€. BUT YOU ARE CALCULATING: 50€ = 1 SHIFT AS A BARTENDER, SO...

~~ONCE~~ FINALLY YOU ARE THERE AND PEOPLE KEEP CHECKING YOUR HOMEPAGE. SEEING THIS SO THEY WANT THIS FOR THEIR MAGAZINE

OUT

FOR DUMMY-MAGAZINE "TEMPO", 2007

YOU DEAL WITH EDITORS, ART DIRECTORS ETC., AND SOMEHOW YOU FIND YOURSELF IN A RELATIONSHIP.
LOOK HERE: I WAS DATING ALEXANDER SEEBERG-ELVERFELDT AND MATTHIAS LAST FOR QUITE AWHILE. WE WENT COLOUR DANCING AT WATERGATE CLUB.
THOSE WERE SOME FUN YEARS.

5 YEARS

RECORDSLEEVES FOR **WATERGATE CLUB** BERLIN

THAT OUTLINE + PAINT BUCKET TURNED OUT TO BE MY MISSIONARY POSITION. BUT THE GOOD THING about BEING AN ILLUSTRATOR IS: THE RELATIONSHIP WITH a CLIENT is VERY OPEN. YOU ARE FREE TO SLUT AROUND. EXPAND YOUR LOVELIFE. TO AVOID BOREDOM AND KEEP THE ROCK: TRY THEM ALL!

COMING UP:
THE
POLYGAMY
OF
BOCK

OR

JOBS OF AN ILLUSTRATOR NAMED FRANK.

1st JOB I did for NEON.

FLÖÖÖT

DAUMEN ~~HOCH~~

YOU GOT

JJ Abrams Ltd. Recycling-Hof

THESE ARE SEVERAL small jobs I DID FOR NEON MAGAZINE.

AWESOME

Some jobs:
THAT'S GOOD, right?!

SO PEOPLE

ALTERSARMUT
80

64

ARMUT durch Jobverlust

Arbeitslos wegen DER KRISE

33

NOW

WOVOR HAST DU ANGST?

KNOW:

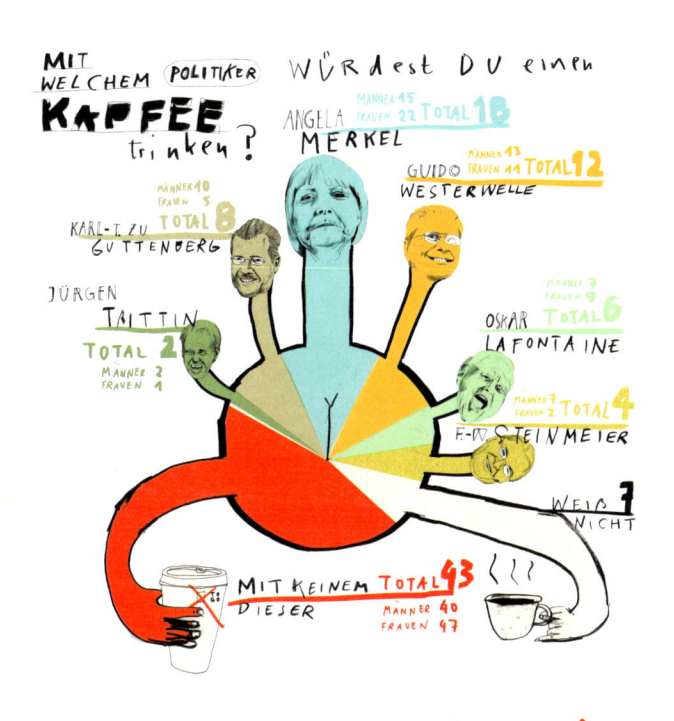

"He is quite ugly, but fast and trustworthy enough to do a bigger job on several pages."

And so I did this for NEON magazine.

MOMENTS OF LOSING BOCK!

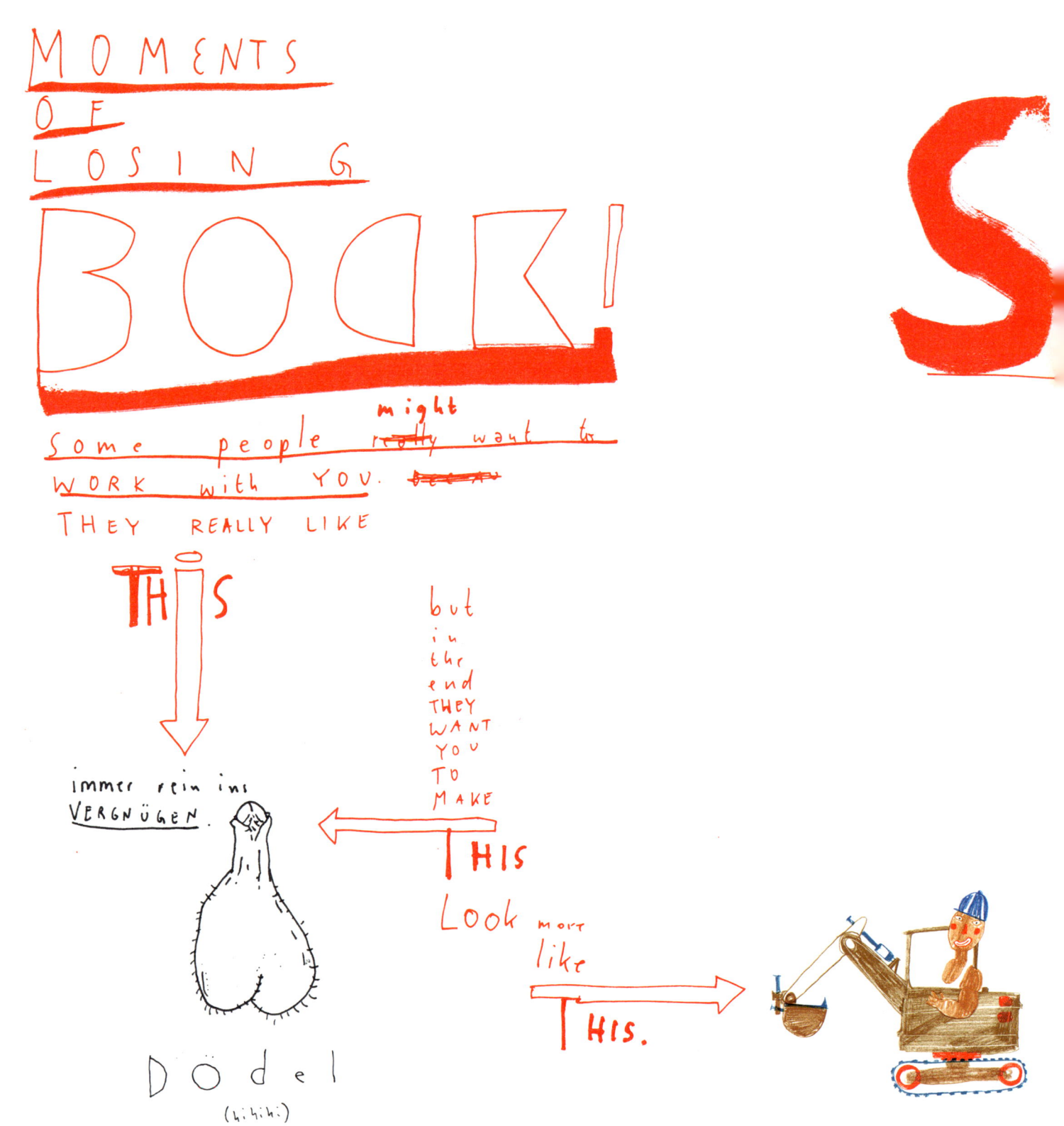

S

Some people might want to WORK WITH YOU. THEY REALLY LIKE

THIS ↓

immer rein ins VERGNÜGEN.

Dödel
(hihihi)

but in the end THEY WANT YOU TO MAKE

THIS Look more like THIS. →

AY NO

to jobs you do not feel comfortable with.

NEVER ~~DON'T~~ Bend your BOCK!

OF COURSE:

AS AN ILLUSTRATOR YOU'RE ONLY PROVIDING A SERVICE. YOU'RE NOT A PHONY ARTIST. BUT STILL: YOU'VE GOT A BRAIN AND YOUR OWN WAY OF EXPRESSING THOUGHTS. SO STICK TO YOUR BOCK when it comes to HOW YOU DO "STUFF".

If you draw.
TRUST YOUR BOCK,
instead of »what people need«.

YOU
will be
surised

Where YOUR ILLUSTRATIONS CAN END UP.

EVEN IF YOU THOUGHT YOUR »STYLE« wouldn't apply to a WOMEN'S MAGAZINE → YOU WORK FOR **BRIGITTE BALANCE**

STILL BRIGITTE BALANCE

ON THAT PAGE.

SORRY.

WOMEN
SEEM TO LIKE IT.

IF YOU (IN GERMANY) MAKE IT IN THE WOMEN'S MAGAZINE FLAGSHIP BRIGITTE →

MONTAG DIENSTAG MITTWOCH DONNERSTAG FREITAG MONTAG.2 MONTAG.1 SAMSTAG SONNTAG?

DIESE MECKEL!
MECKEL
POST PRESSDRÜSE FACH
WAS MACH ICH HIER?

WIRKLICH DRINGEND!!! sind nur
24
7 tage WOCHE → RUHEPHASEN

0:1
Buuuh!
0:1!!! NEHMEN.
EIGENTOR
FOLG
HALTET IHN
DOKTORE

IT'S A BIG HONOUR BECAUSE THIS PROVES THAT
Even a quirky Illustrator like YOU is universally compatible.

HOORAY!

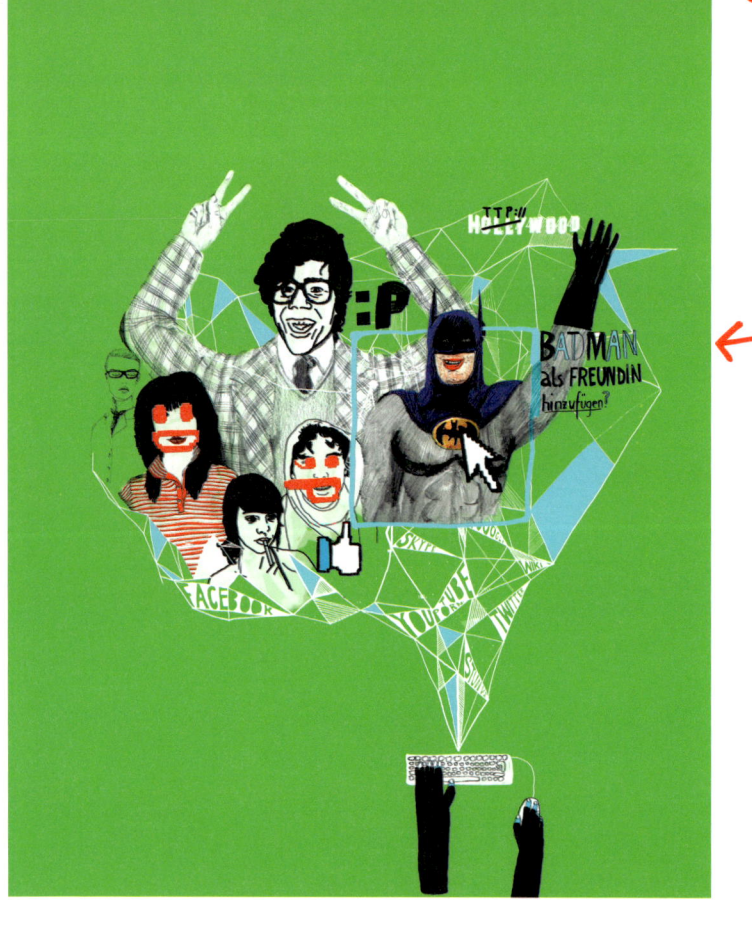

THEN YOU EVEN CAN DO THE COVER and 3 DOUBLEPAGES FOR CHRISMON, THE GERMAN PROTESTANTS' MAGAZINE.

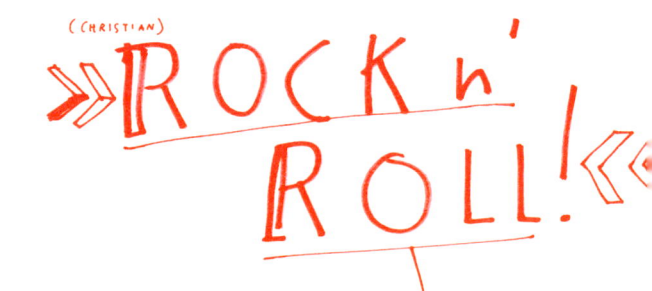

(CHRISTIAN) ROCK n' ROLL!

MARRY ME
SWINGER
JOY CLUB
SINGLES
SCHMECKEN
RIECHEN
die ECHTE WELT STINKT,
UND DAS IST
GUT
SO!
FÜHLEN
FREE MEMBERSHIP
SEHEN
HTTP://
WEB
PREMIUM

B
QUELLE: INTERNET
DAS RAD
KOHLEFADEN LAMPE
COMPUTER
KONRAD ZUSE
Z1
KAFFEE MASCHINE
INTERNET
4000 v. Chr.
1879
1938
1954
1969
2010
EVENTEINLADUNG
geil, ich bring bier mit. freu
supi. was n mit daniel?
daniel spielt bestimmt mit seinem rad. rofl!
DANIEL
VIELLEICHT ROLL ICH DAS RAD NOCHN BISSL DURCH DIE HÖHLE?

YOU

YOU DRAW EVERYDAY FROM

THAT SUCK(S)

but WHY?

realize:

9 AM → 5 PM or even LOOOOng

isn't IT COOL TO MAKE MONEY with YOUR HOBBY? — WELL, is it ever. COOL TO WRITE THIS TEXT SLANTED? — WELL, WHAT WHY? — WELL, YOU?

DOWNSIDE OF BEING A BUSY ILLUSTRATOR:

YOUR BRAIN!

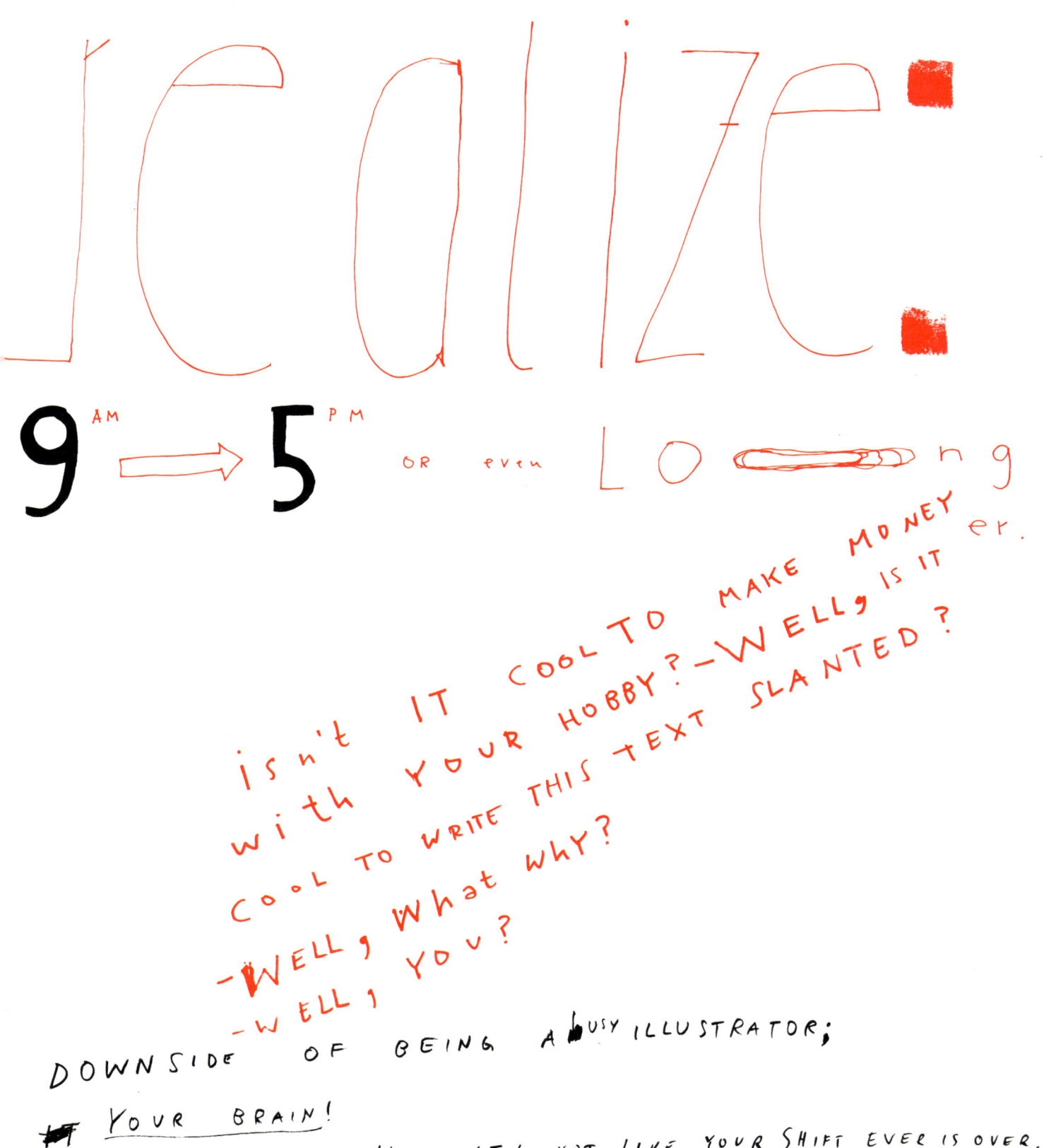

DELIVERing IDEAS all the time. IT'S NOT LIKE YOUR SHIFT EVER IS OVER. YOU'RE WORKING ALL the TIME. YOU TRY TO RELAX AND SUDDENLY YOU HAVE AN IDEA FOR THE JOB.
SO YOU MAKE MONEY WITH → YOUR THOUGHTS.

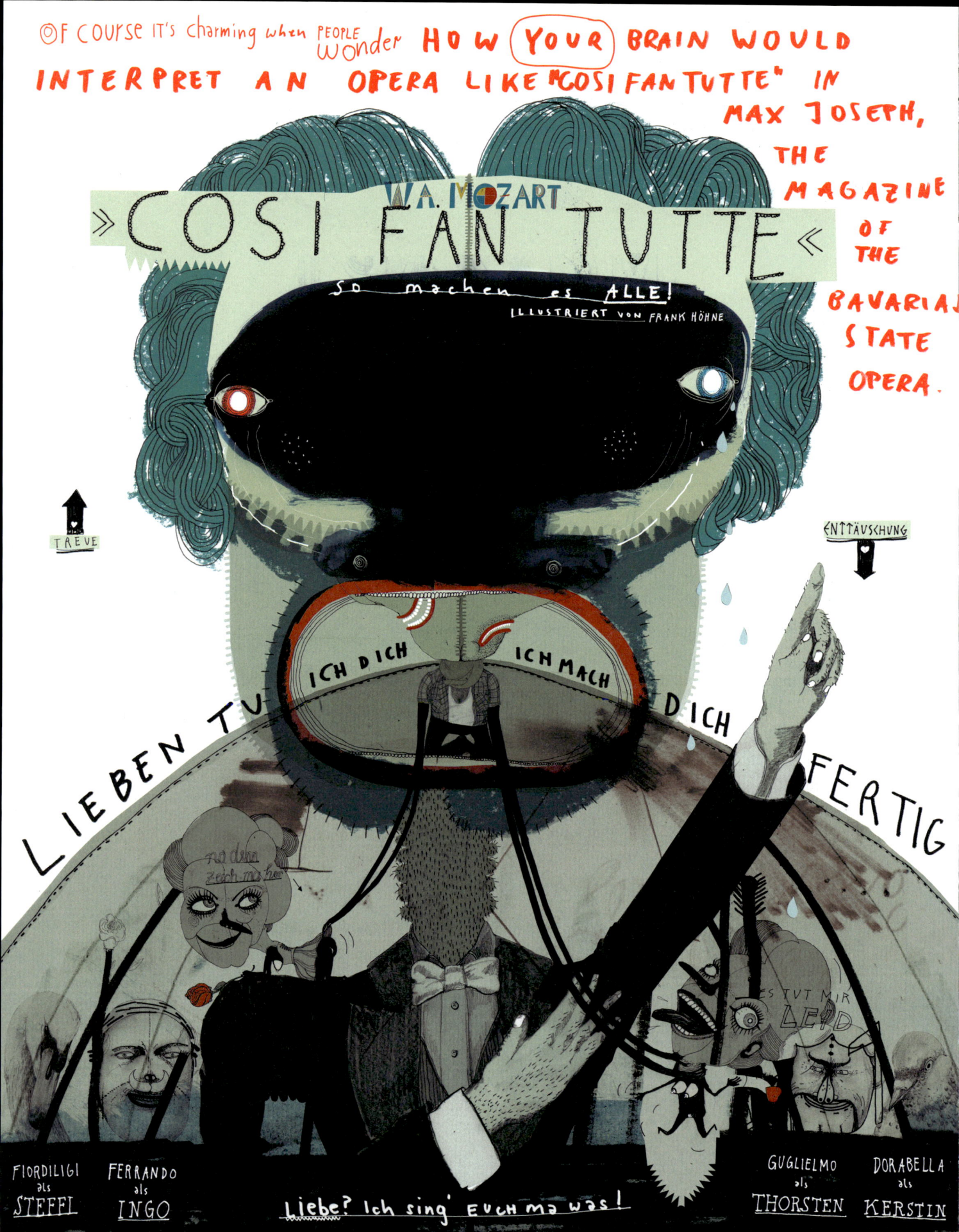

Of course it's charming when people wonder how (your) brain would interpret an opera like "Cosi fan tutte" in Max Joseph, the magazine of the Bavarian State Opera.

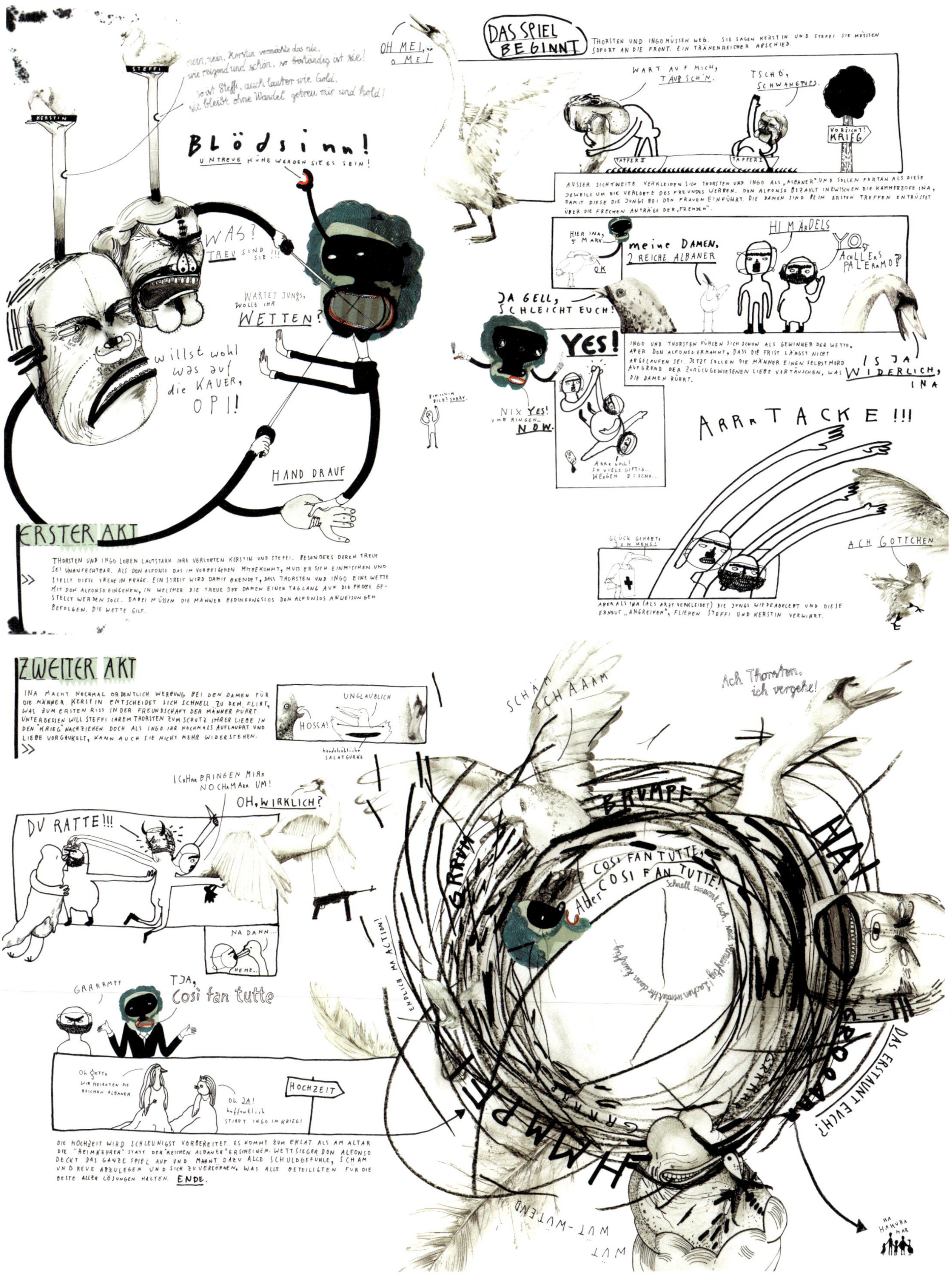

STEFFI
KERSTIN
nein, nein, Kerstin vermöchte das nie,
wie reizend und schön, so beständig ist sie!
so ist Steffi, auch lauter wie Gold,
sie bleibt ohne Wandel getreu mir und hold!
Blödsinn!
UNTREUE KÜHE WERDEN SIE ES SEIN!
WAS? TREU SIND SIE!!!
WARTET JUNGS, WOLLT IHR WETTEN?
willst wohl was auf die KAUER, OPI!
HAND DRAUF
ERSTER AKT
THORSTEN UND INGO LOBEN LAUTSTARK IHRE VERLOBTEN KERSTIN UND STEFFI. BESONDERS DEREN TREUE SEI UNANFECHTBAR. ALS DON ALFONSO DAS IM VORBEIGEHEN MITBEKOMMT, MUSS ER SICH EINMISCHEN UND STELLT DIESE TREUE IN FRAGE. EIN STREIT WIRD DAMIT BEENDET, DASS THORSTEN UND INGO EINE WETTE MIT DON ALFONSO EINGEHEN, IN WELCHER DIE TREUE DER DAMEN EINEN TAG LANG AUF DIE PROBE GESTELLT WERDEN SOLL. DABEI MÜSSEN DIE MÄNNER BEDINGUNGSLOS DON ALFONSOS ANWEISUNGEN BEFOLGEN. DIE WETTE GILT.
>>
OH MEI, O MEI
DAS SPIEL BEGINNT
THORSTEN UND INGO MÜSSEN WEG. SIE SAGEN KERSTIN UND STEFFI SIE MÜSSTEN SOFORT AN DIE FRONT. EIN TRÄNENREICHER ABSCHIED.
WART AUF MICH, TÄUBSCH'N.
TSCHÖ, SCHWANEPUPS.
VORSICHT! KRIEG
TAPFER II
TAPFER I
AUSSER SICHTWEITE VERKLEIDEN SICH THORSTEN UND INGO ALS „ALBANER". UND SOLLEN FORTAN ALS DIESE JEWEILS UM DIE VERLOBTE DES FREUNDES WERBEN. DON ALFONSO BEZAHLT INZWISCHEN DIE KAMMERZOFE INA, DAMIT DIESE DIE JUNGS BEI DEN FRAUEN EINFÜHRT. DIE DAMEN SIND BEIM ERSTEN TREFFEN ENTRÜSTET ÜBER DIE FRECHEN ANTRÄGE DER „FREMDEN".
HIER INA, 5 MARK
OK
meine DAMEN, 2 REICHE ALBANER
HI MÄRDELS
YO, ACHLLERS PALERMO?
JA GELL, SCHLEICHT EUCH!
YES!
NIX YES!
NOW.
INGO UND THORSTEN FÜHLEN SICH SCHON ALS GEWINNER DER WETTE. ABER DON ALFONSO ERMAHNT, DASS DIE FRIST LÄNGST NICHT ABGELAUFEN SEI. JETZT SOLLEN DIE MÄNNER EINEN SELBSTMORD AUFGRUND DER ZURÜCKGEWIESENEN LIEBE VORTÄUSCHEN, WAS DIE DAMEN RÜHRT.
IS JA WIDERLICH, INA
ARRRTACKE!!!
GLÜCK GEHABT, JUNKENS!
ACH GOTTCHEN
ABER ALS INA (ALS ARZT VERKLEIDET) DIE JUNGS WIEDERBELEBT UND DIESE ERNEUT „ANGREIFEN", FLIEHEN STEFFI UND KERSTIN VERWIRRT.
ZWEITER AKT
INA MACHT NOCHMAL ORDENTLICH WERBUNG BEI DEN DAMEN FÜR DIE MÄNNER. KERSTIN ENTSCHEIDET SICH SCHNELL ZU DEM FLIRT, WAS ZUM ERSTEN RISS IN DER FREUNDSCHAFT DER MÄNNER FÜHRT. UNTERDESSEN WILL STEFFI IHREM THORSTEN ZUM SCHUTZ IHRER LIEBE IN DEN "KRIEG" NACHZIEHEN. DOCH ALS INGO IHR NOCHMALS AUFLAUERT UND LIEBE VORGAUKELT, KANN AUCH SIE NICHT MEHR WIDERSTEHEN.
>>
UNGLAUBLICH
HOSSA!
handelsübliche SALATGURKE
SCHÄM SCHAAAM
Ach Thorsten, ich vergehe!
ICHRR BRINGEN MIRR NOCHRMARR UM!
OH, WIRKLICH?
DU RATTE!!!
NA DANN...
HEHE..
GRRRRMPF
TJA, Cosi fan tutte
Oh Gott, WIR HEIRATEN DIE REICHEN ALBANER
Oh JA! hoffentlich STIRBT INGO IM KRIEG!
HOCHZEIT
DIE HOCHZEIT WIRD SCHLEUNIGST VORBEREITET. ES KOMMT ZUM EKLAT ALS AM ALTAR DIE "HEIMKEHRER" STATT DER "REICHEN ALBANER" ERSCHEINEN. WETTSIEGER DON ALFONSO DECKT DAS GANZE SPIEL AUF UND MAHNT DAZU ALLE SCHULDGEFÜHLE, SCHAM UND REUE ABZULEGEN UND SICH ZU VERSÖHNEN, WAS ALLE BETEILIGTEN FÜR DIE BESTE ALLER LÖSUNGEN HALTEN. ENDE.
ENDLICH MA ACTION!
BRUMPF
GRRRR
HA!
COSI FAN TUTTE,
Aber COSI FAN TUTTE!
DAS ERSTAUNT EUCH?
WUT WUT-WÜTEND
HA HAHUHA HAR

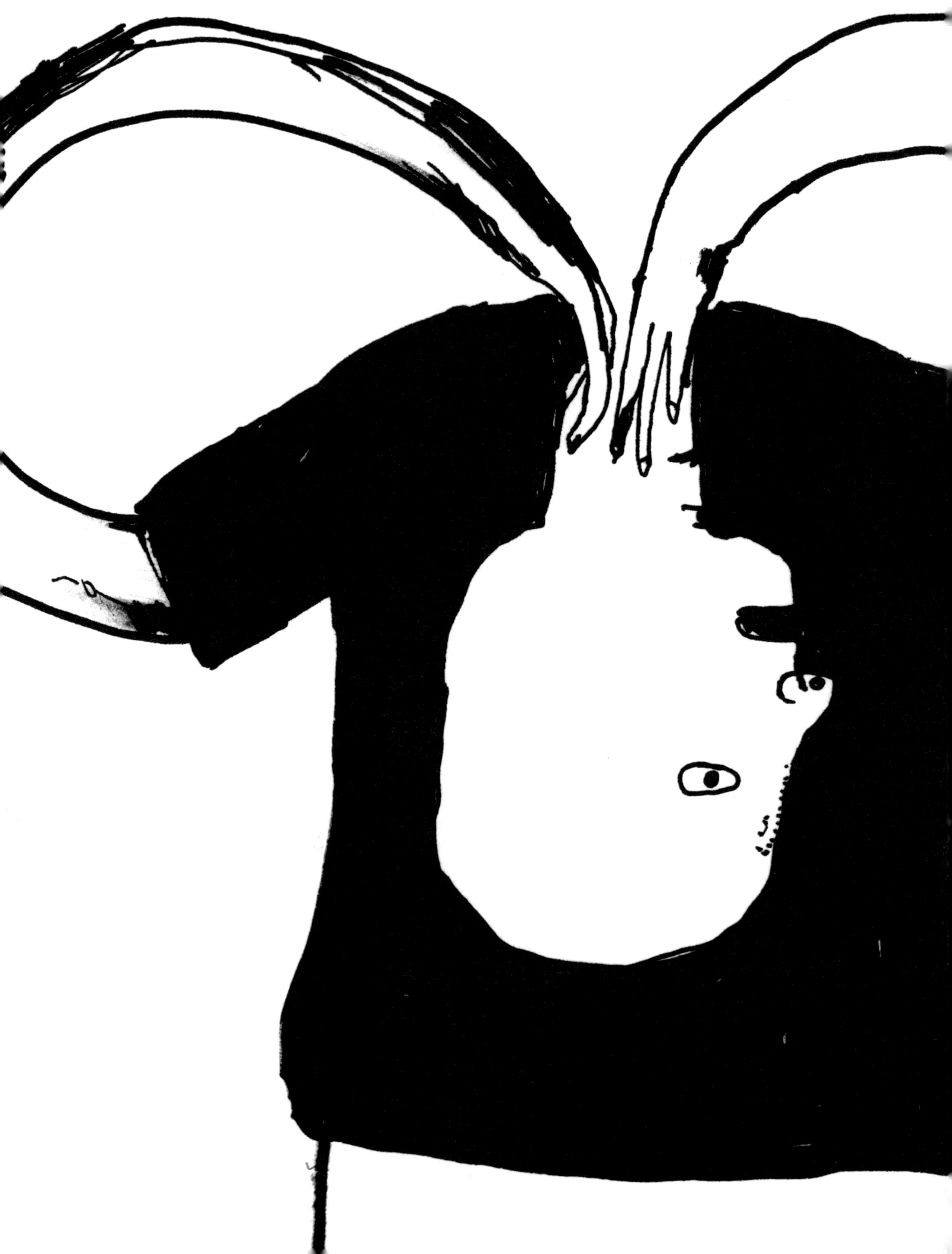

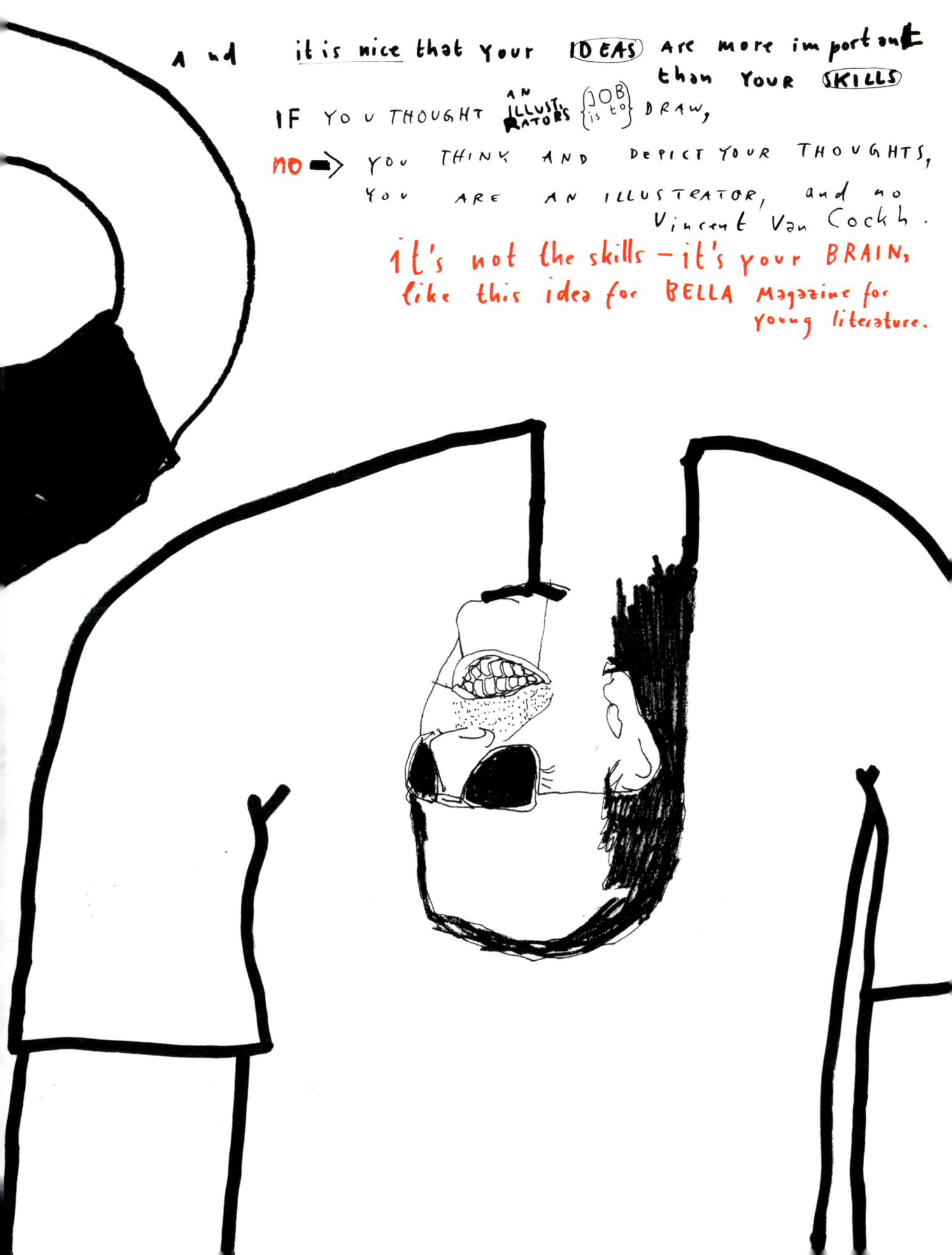

And it is nice that your IDEAS are more important than your SKILLS. IF YOU THOUGHT AN ILLUSTRATORS JOB IS TO DRAW, no → YOU THINK AND DEPICT YOUR THOUGHTS, YOU ARE AN ILLUSTRATOR, and no Vincent Van Cockh.

it's not the skills — it's your BRAIN, like this idea for BELLA Magazine for young literature.

BUT

IDEAS
IDEALS
IDIET ~~IDET~~
IDIOT

→ DIE WHAT YOU HAVE TO COME ~~DO~~ UP WITH

→ DIE WHAT YOU HAVE.
YOU WANT TO HAVE GOOD AND UNIQUE IDEAS.

→ IS WHAT YOUR BRAIN FEELS LIKE. I = YOUR BRAIN } THE LONGER YOU WORK, THE
DIET = DIET } MORE IDEAS YOU NEED
YOU FEEL SHRINKAGE IN YOUR BRAIN, LIKE EACH IDEA YOU SELL IS ONE KILOGRAM OF YOUR THOUGHTS. <u>AND YOU FEAR</u>

being an
→ <u>i D I O T</u>

Imagine YOU RAN OUT OF IDEAS. <u>YOU HAVE NO IDEAS LEFT</u> → because you iDIEted too long. YOUR BRAIN LOOKS LIKE A MODEL BUT THINKS THE SAME..

ONCE IN A (HI HI) WHALE

I AM A TEENAGE-MUTANT-HERO-TURDLE

YOU NEED TO ☒ ☒ FLUSH YOUR CACHÉ

(GET THE SERIOUS SHIT OUT OF YOUR LITTLE BUCKET)

it's all about

WORK ⸺⸺⸺⸺⸺⸺⸺⸺⸺ BOCK

BALAhce

YOU WORK FOR EXAMPLE

NEON MAGAZINE

AFTER THAT MUCH "THINKING" YOU DEFINITELY HAVE TO FLUSH YOUR BRAIN BY DOING SOMETHING THAT MAKES YOU FEEL

BOCK.

just like →

drew "some" THING

"something like some GUY"

I mean anything without THINKING.

with coloured PENcils

feeding HIS HORSE WITH AN APPLE BURGER

Or FINELINERS

WHY NOT?

HEU
UREKA
BAM
BLOKY
SCHÖN VERTEILEN
HONIG
KOPFEL
KATHRIN? OJE. WIE TRAURIG!
WAT TRAURIG!! LERN DU ERSMA POMMES.
DIE LEUTE KUKKEN MICH AN, SIE MÖGEN DAS

OR take a paper and fill IT WITH WHAT EVER YOU HAVE BOCK for

MANN mit Ideen, aber ohne HAUT, daher untauglich für den Außendienst

because that is the solution to your work problem.

TRAM
NACH HAUSE. ABER IN DER STRASSENBAHN, DIE
HINTER IHNEN FUHR, WAR ZUGFÜHRER EBEN JENER SCHAFFNER, DER EINST DEN MANTEL DES GEIGERS AUF DEM FLOHMARKT
VERKAUFT HATTE. UND SO FAHREN SIE SPÄT ABENDS DURCH DIE STADT: VORNWEG DER GEIGER
DER GEIGER, VERWIRRT ÜBER DEN

or: draw some city with pencils and if you got enough **BOCK** → colour it afterwards

I haven't GOT any BOCK left for that — but that's OK = YOU KNOW → I am HUMAN

SO TO KEEP THE BOOK WHEN YOU WORK AS AN ILLUSTRACTOR

You need to be free enough to do your own stuff outside of THE JOB. THAT MEANS YOU NEED TO EARN ENOUGH MONEY TO PAY YOUR RENT AND TO KEEP YOUR FAMILY AND YOURSELF BUSY ON THE TOILET

Norbert, 49, beim klauen / Norbert, 49, while stealing

Muss mEine FAMILIE irgendwie am KACKEN halten

Voll mit PRODUKTEN

AND + enough to take A DAY OR MORE OFF from JOB-WORK to BOCK-WORK.

YOU won't get rich as an illustraitor

So do not TRY IT. YOU can work your A** OFF AND LOSE YOUR BOCK

FAIL!

OR:

~~THE~~ YOUR CONCEPT OF WORKING (earning money) is TO AFFORD **NOT TO WORK**.

You work that much, that you can survive and enjoy the DAYS OFF when you can BOCK-UP your LIFE with STUFF you always wanted to do. like: EXAMPLE →

* 29. December 1800
† 1. Juli 1860
CHARLES NELSON
1839
Durch einen »wissenschaftlichen Zufall« ENTDECKT GOODYEAR GUMMI
DIE REIFENPRÜFUNG
FRANK SEIBERLING
"Mr GOODYEAR
you're trying to seduce me... aren't you?"
Tire & Rubber company
1898
GRÜNDUNG DER GOODYEAR TIRE & RUBBER COMPANY, BENANNT NACH CHARLES GOODYEAR, DEM BEGRÜNDER DER MODERNEN GUMMI-INDUSTRIE.
CHARLES SEIBERLING
Akron / Ohio
1901
GOODYEAR
produziert erstmals AUTOREIFEN
henry FORD
Ford T
1916
GOODYEAR
wird der größte Reifenhersteller weltweit
ON THE WINGS OF GOODYEAR
GOODYEAR
1910 KANADA
1927 ENGLAND
1954 GRÜNDUNG Deutsche GOODYEAR GmbH
DEUTSCHLAND
1898 AKRON / Ohio
USA
GRÜNDUNG GOODYEAR Tire & Rubber Company
1999
GOODYEAR + DUNLOP
JOINT VENTURE
GOODYEAR DUNLOP GmbH
PATENTAMT
Luftreifen
Schottland
1888
John Boyd (Tierarzt) DUNLOP
1889 Gründung des 1sten Reifenwerks der DUNLOP-Gruppe
1893 1ste AUSLANDSNIEDERLASSUNG IN HANAU / BRD
you work for DUNLOP germany
OK. Monday → Tuesday

Wednesday → Thursday

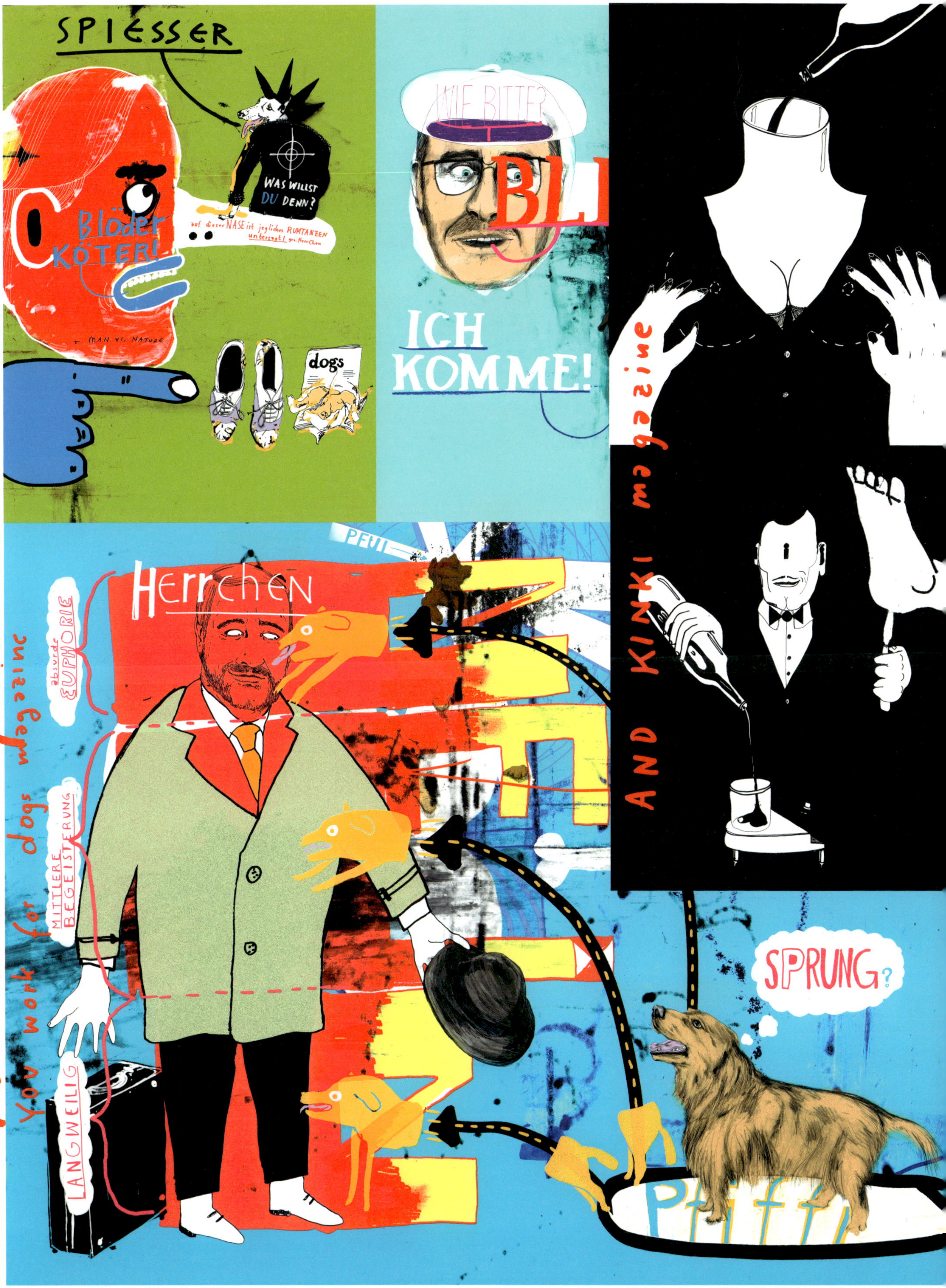

and FRIDAY or rather THE REST OF THE MONTH

You u work
for free
because
you like
some → magazine

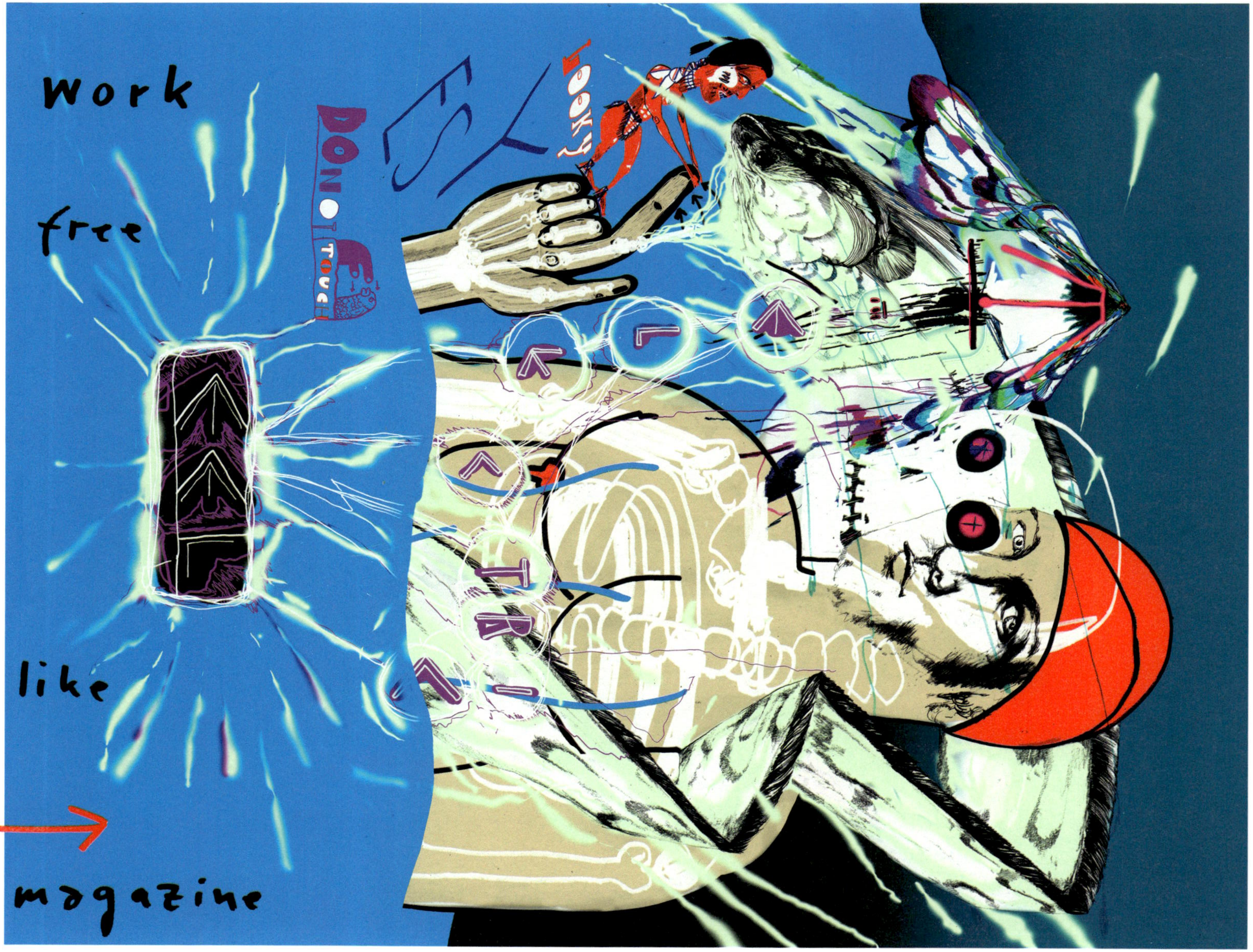

OR YOU DO PROJECTS WITH FRIENDS LIKE

Musik ist tot

HORT

SOME TIME ON SK
SPEND
OR YOU

ALLES
IST
SPANNEND,
SOBALD
WAS PIMMELÄHNLICHES
DEN ~~DEN~~ RAUM
betritt

ANYTHING GETS EXCITING
AS SOON AS SOMETHING
DICK-LIKE ENTERS
THE ROOM

ETCHBOOKS AGAIN

IF YOU DOUBT YOUR BOOK FOR ~~LIVING~~ BEING AN ILLUSTRATOR IT ALWAYS HELPS TO REMEMBER WHERE YOU COME FROM. I DID SO MANY SKETCHBOOKS AND DIDN'T FIND THE TIME, BUT WHEN I TAKE THE TIME TO DO IT NOW, I REMEMBER WHY I ~~GOT~~ UNO ILLUSTRATORE BECAME. BOOK, BABY, BOOK. —BOCK.

Gilt auch für TITTEN

ALSO APPLIES TO TITTIES.

OR
remember
RAVE BRAIN
doggy
ICH, PFERD,
hab den Kopf voller SAUEREIEN
KACKE!
do

SAFE

12

how much you liked to MAKE collages OUT OF your material (without meaning)?

that.

FIND TO do CAN

TIME some for your living room.

DR VAS

SCARrrRYY iiech

it doesn't matter
what you do to keep
up the big BOCK as an
ILLUSTRIPPER.

BUT: **never**
feel like you're
finished.
ALWAYS EXPLORE NEW
THINGS. TRY and TRY
and TRY. THERE is
so much BOCK in this
world.
if you feel like you're finished it means your EARTH-work is done.
YOUR ~~and~~
MIND, HEART & SOUL NEED TO BE BUSY ~~instead of~~
SO KEEP ON BEGINNING,
when you feel an end coming up.

if you are tired of drawing try something else in between that you haven't done yet.

EVEN THE BEST RELATIONSHIPS NEED AFFAIRS NOW AND THEN TO MAKE YOU REALIZE HOW AMAZING SHE IS.

SO HAVE INSPIRATIONAL QUICHIES WITH EVERY OFFER TO MAKE YOUR PEN-MARRIAGE LAST

I understand

FOREVER

POSSIBLE QUICKIE:

YOU crochet friends

THRANK
YOU
very much.

for your
FAMILY.

OR

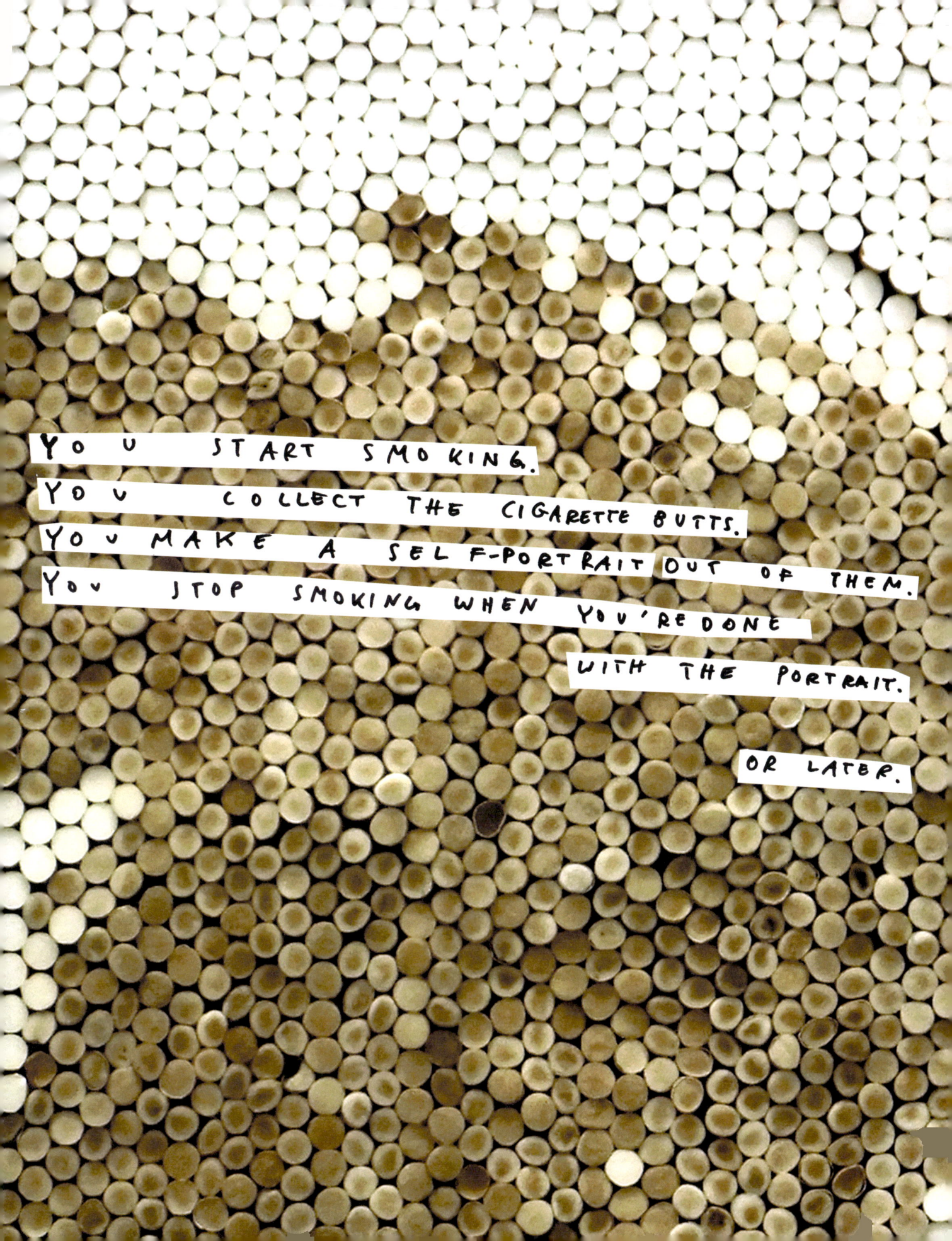

YOU START SMOKING.
YOU COLLECT THE CIGARETTE BUTTS.
YOU MAKE A SELF-PORTRAIT OUT OF THEM.
YOU STOP SMOKING WHEN YOU'RE DONE
WITH THE PORTRAIT.

OR LATER.

OR: You can always write a song about IT!

OH THANK DOG, final PAGE.
YOU THOUGHT THIS CRAP WOULD NEVER END, right? BUT HERE WE ARE.
TIME FOR ANOTHER STUPID PIECE OF ADVICE:

LIFE IS A FRAGILE TOY — SO TAKE CARE
BUT PLAY!

AND ANOTHER ONE (RÉSUMÉ):

BOCK is a REWARD
FOR BEING FRANK WITH YOURSELF and this planet.

THANK YOU, EUer FRANK

The Book of Bock
FRANK HÖHNE

Cover by Frank Höhne
Layout by Frank Höhne

Project management by Elisabeth Honerla for Gestalten
Production management by Vinzenz Geppert for Gestalten
Proofread by Transparent Language Solutions
Printed by Livonia Print, Riga
Made in EUROPE

Published by Gestalten, Berlin 2012
ISBN 978-3-89955-456-4

© Die Gestalten Verlag GmbH & Co. KG, Berlin 2012
All rights reserved. No part of this publication may be reproduced or transmitted in any form or by any means, electronic or mechanical, including photocopy or any storage and retrieval system, without permission in writing from the publisher.
RESPECT COPYRIGHTS, ENCOURAGE CREATIVITY!
For more information, please visit www.gestalten.com.
Bibliographic information published by the Deutsche Nationalbibliothek.
THE DEUTSCHE NATIONALBIBLIOTHEK lists this publication in the Deutsche Nationalbibliografie; detailed bibliographic data are available online at http://dnb.d-nb.de.

This BOOK was printed on paper certified by the FSC®.

MIX
Paper from responsible sources
FSC® C002795

Gestalten is a climate-neutral company. We collaborate with the non-profit carbon offset provider myclimate (www.myclimate.org) to neutralize the company's carbon footprint produced through our worldwide business activities by investing in projects that reduce CO_2 emissions (www.gestalten.com/myclimate).

myclimate
Protect our planet